Victorian Staffordshire Dogs

A. and N. Harding

Schiffer Publishing Ltd.

80 Lower Valley Road, Atglen, PA 19310 USA

Dedication

This book is dedicated to Staffordshire figure collectors everywhere.

Other Schiffer Books by A. & N. Harding
Victorian Staffordshire Figures 1835-1875, Book One, Portraits, Naval & Military, Theatrical & Literary Charaters.
Victorian Staffordshire Figures 1835-1875, Book Two, Religious, Hunters, Pastoral, Occupations, Children & Animals, Dogs, Animals, Cottages & Castles, Sport & Miscellaneous.
Victorian Staffordshire Figures, 1835-1875, Book Three.
Victorian Staffordshire Figures, 1875-1962.

Other Schiffer Books on Related Subjects
Staffordshire Spaniels, Adele Kenny.
Staffordshire Animals: A Collector's Guide to History, Styles, and Values, Adele Kenny.
Staffordshire Figures, Adele Kenny & Veronica Moriarty.

Copyright © 2006 by A. & N. Harding
Library of Congress Control Number: 2006921732

Designed by John P. Cheek
Cover design by Bruce Waters
Type set in Bodoni Bd BT/Aldine 721 BT

ISBN: 0-7643-2456-X
Printed in China

Published by Schiffer Publishing Ltd.
4880 Lower Valley Road
Atglen, PA 19310
Phone: (610) 593-1777; Fax: (610) 593-2002
E-mail: Info@schifferbooks.com

For the largest selection of fine reference books on this and related subjects, please visit our web site at
www.schifferbooks.com
We are always looking for people to write books on new and related subjects. If you have an idea for a book please contact us at the above address.

This book may be purchased from the publisher.
Include $3.95 for shipping.
Please try your bookstore first.
You may write for a free catalog.

In Europe, Schiffer books are distributed by
Bushwood Books
6 Marksbury Ave.
Kew Gardens
Surrey TW9 4JF England
Phone: 44 (0) 20 8392-8585;
Fax: 44 (0) 20 8392-9876
E-mail: info@bushwoodbooks.co.uk
Website: www.bushwoodbooks.co.uk
Free postage in the U.K., Europe; air mail at cost.

Contents

Acknowledgments 4

Introduction 5

Chapter One. Dogs 18

Chapter Two. Dogs with Children 134

Chapter Three. Dogs with Their Masters 178

Index 255

Acknowledgments

The authors wish to thank those collectors and dealers who allowed their stock and collections to be photographed for illustration in this book.

The authors may be contacted by mail or in person at:

Scadbury Stables
Southfleet
Kent
England
DA13 9PP
Telephone +44(0) 147483 4120 or +44(0) 7887 885988

Or you may visit our website at www. staffordshirefigures.com or E-mail us at nick@staffordshirefigures.com

Introduction

From the early 1900s up until the 1950s, the collecting of Victorian Staffordshire figures was unheard of and would have been deemed an eccentric pastime. For a long time, the realisation that they were one of the last English folk arts was sadly overlooked. At the end of the Second World War, when the visiting sailors, soldiers, and air crews returned home, it was to the United States and Canada that thousands of these figures were taken as mementoes of their stay in England. The exodus of figures continued when American tourists returned after the war.

At the time they were considered inexpensive, being recognised as typical of an age that had long since passed. Most of these figures have stayed in North America, today forming some of the finest collections in existence.

It was not until the 1960s that the situation in the United Kingdom changed. In that decade, some of the greatest collections were formed, including Balston, Pugh, Owen, and Bloomfield, all of which are now dispersed or given over to museums. Victorian Staffordshire figures had finally achieved the appreciation that they so justly deserved in their own homeland.

The collecting of Victorian Staffordshire figures is now firmly established, and never again will we see them dismissed as mere 'pottery chimney ornaments'. The prices now realised for the rarest and the best compare to and exceed the prices paid for porcelain figures made at the same time. The prices for our unknown potters' works often exceeds that of marked Dresden, Meissen, and other Continental factories' figures.

Books

In 1955 Mr R. Hagger's book, *Staffordshire Chimney Ornaments* was published. This text was followed closely in 1958 by Mr Thomas Balston's book entitled *Staffordshire Portrait Figures of the Victorian Age*. This book illustrated, for the first time, a quite comprehensive catalogue of the Portrait figures that had been made.

These two publications led to an increased interest and awareness of this forgotten art. Soon articles on the figures began to appear in magazines and periodicals, with other smaller books on specific themes also published. These books and periodicals revived interest in Victorian Staffordshire figures as an art form and in 1970, P. D Gordon Pugh's *Staffordshire Figures of the Victorian Era* was published. It contained pictures and information on over 1300 portrait figures. This publication was complimented in 1971 by Anthony Oliver's book, *The Victorian Staffordshire Figure*. In 1981 Anthony Oliver followed the success of his first book with another titled, *Staffordshire Pottery The Tribal Art of England*.

Due in part to the revived interest in Victorian Staffordshire figures, and the ever increasing prices, auction houses began to hold regular sales devoted entirely to Staffordshire figures. Previously, unless a particularly large collection was for sale, these figures were included with the general pottery and porcelain sales.

In 1990, the late Clive Mason Pope published privately *A – Z of Staffordshire Dogs*. This was the first time any attempt had been made to catalogue other than portrait figures, and it was mainly for the American market that this book was published, for it was this market that first realised the importance and collectability of decorative figures and in particular dogs and dog groups.

With the publication in 1998 of the two volumes of *Victorian Staffordshire Figures 1835-1875*, we attempted to catalogue all aspects of Victorian Staffordshire figure production, concentrating not just on Portraiture or dogs, but including the many other categories which had been made. The entire range of figures were included, figures which had in the past been neglected. Among the neglected figures were Animals, Cottages, Religious, and the many types of Decorative figures.

The year 2000 saw the publication of our *Book Three The Addendum*, which supplemented the first two volumes and added a further 1,100 or so figures to the catalogues.

The year 2003 saw the publication of our book *Victorian Staffordshire Figures 1875-1962*, which catalogued all the later figures until the closure of the last pottery making these figures in 1962. As these previous books contain over 4,000 illustrated figures, the dogs and allied figures are spread over four volumes. This book brings together all those figures in which the dog is either the figure or is an important part of the figure. This volume has added nearly 300 figures that were not in the previous four volumes.

Every book published on this nineteenth century folk art should add to our knowledge and understanding, knowledge that is still surprisingly scant. The potters kept few written records of their work, and virtually none have survived the past one hundred and fifty years.

Figures Included

The task of compiling a definitive and exhaustive catalogue of Staffordshire dogs may never be completed, as we are still finding new examples. We do believe that with this book, the **majority** of collectable figures that have **survived** the last 150 years have now been catalogued.

This still leaves the **minority.** Whilst difficult to be precise, from our experience and knowledge we would estimate there to be at least another 200 to 300 **collectable** figures still to be found and photographed. With the help of collectors and dealers alike, some time in the future a second edition may contain them.

There are also many small figures of two to six inches in height that were made in their thousands, all of little merit, usually poorly coloured, if coloured at all. These are generally badly modelled, often because the potter used the mould for too many figures, thus producing inferior ones. Many of these figures have survived and can be purchased for relatively small sums.

These smaller figures were made in their thousands for very little cost, and it is probable that they would have been given away at fairs as prizes. This type of prize was known as a 'fairing'. Figures other than these were relatively more expensive to produce and would not have been given away. Unfortunately, because some were 'fairings', this word is sometimes applied incorrectly to all Staffordshire figures.

Figures such as these have not been included in this book as most collectors avoid them. The Victorians created many thousands of wonderful oil paintings, but also painted thousands of little or no quality; the same applies to Staffordshire figures.

Figure Numbers

The figure number given to each figure is the same number that appears in our previous four volumes. Where the figure is a new addition, the number allocated to it will correspond to past volumes and cataloguing for future editions.

Prices

As with most antiques, the quality and condition of a Staffordshire figure does vary, and no two are exactly alike. The price paid for a piece will not only reflect this, but also where it was bought. A figure is likely to be more expensive if it is purchased from a specialist dealer, with a large stock from which to choose, and willing to offer advice and detail any repair or restoration. A figure may be considerably less expensive when purchased from a market stall where the figure is part of a general stock, the trader knowing little or nothing about it.

In the authors' opinions, auction prices are not a reliable guide. In the past there have been numerous occasions when figures at auction have realised high prices, which have not been sustained.

There are a number of reasons for this situation:

Private purchasers may not realise that they are bidding against a high or unrealistic reserve.

It takes only two bidders intent on acquiring a particular figure for the price to escalate.

'Auction fever', which can occur when bidders drawn by the occasion and a persuasive auctioneer pay a price, which is later regretted.

Prices at auction continue to reach record levels, levels that if sustained and carried through to other figures of equal merit will take many figures beyond the means of most. This trend, whilst disturbing, and cold comfort to collectors wishing to add to their collections, will no doubt be of great satisfaction to those who collected figures whilst prices were relatively low.

Wild animals, figures with sporting connections, very rare portrait figures, and rare dog groups and pairs are now at the top of the market with four figure prices being paid. In most instances they are at last realising what most Staffordshire collectors knew to be their true value when compared to other, equivalent antiques.

Listed below are a selection of figures, with their guide price, and final selling price that has been achieved at auction in England in the last few years:

Description	Fig. No.	Estimate	Price paid
A pair of pointers	2698/2699	£500-£800	£3646
A pair of seated pugs	2779/2780	£200-£300	£1152
A pair of seated spaniels on malachite bases	2530/2531	£1200-£1800	£2940
A pair of children standing below large red and white dogs	2221/2222	£600-£800	£2687
A pair of spill vase figures of children asleep with dogs protecting them from snakes	2227/2228	£200-£300	£1875
A pair of seated spaniels on cushion bases	2563/2564	£200-£300	£1250
A pair of large red and white dogs on scrolled bases	2716/2717	£1000-£1200	£3450

There are however, in the author's opinion, still bargains to be found. Decorative figures of huntsmen and shepherds with their dogs, either singularly or in pairs, can all still be purchased for less than £1000.00 ($1800) and most for less than £500.00 ($900) and at this price they can be found perfect and extremely rare.

Price Guide

Within This Price Guide

Against each figure, a **GUIDE** price has been given. We must **EMPHASISE** that this is not necessarily the price for the figure illustrated. If the figure is pristine or unique, it is likely to be **ABOVE** the higher guide price.

A figure of good quality, in reasonable condition with minor restoration or minor repair, should be found **WITHIN** the price guide.

A heavily restored figure or one of poor quality should be purchased **BELOW** the lower price guide.

The **GUIDE** prices shown below have been given in two currencies, Pounds Sterling and U.S. Dollars. Prices for Staffordshire figures in the United Kingdom are generally lower than prices in the United States, so it is difficult to give a direct price conversion.

£	Pounds Sterling	$	U.S Dollars
A+	£4000.00 +	A+	$10000.00 +
A	£3000.00 to £4000.00	A	$8000.00 to $10000.00
B	£2000.00 to £3000.00	B	$5000.00 to $8000.00
C	£1000.00 to £2000.00	C	$3000.00 to $5000.00
D	£500.00 to £1000.00	D	$1500.00 to $3000.00
E	£300.00 to £500.00	E	$1000.00 to $1500.00
F	£150.00 to £300.00	F	$600.00 to $1000.00
G	£50.00 to £150.00	G	$200.00 to $650.00
H	£ Below £50	H	$ Below $200.00

Sizes

The size of each figure is given to the nearest quarter inch, but the same figure can vary in size up to half an inch, usually due to the size of the base. Where the authors are aware of more than one size, each measurement has been given. **This is not definitive and other sizes of figures do exist.**

Buying and Selling

Over the course of 150 years, for most of which Staffordshire figures were regarded as nothing more than cheap decorations, and for the most part treated with contempt, it is therefore surprising that so many figures have survived. Many, if not most, of the figures have suffered degrees of damage; in particular, the overglaze enamels

are prone to flaking, so examples that have survived in pristine condition are a rarity. When figures of this nature are offered for sale they do command a premium.

For a figure to be classed pristine, in order of importance it must be: -

Perfect.

No damage, no restoration, no repair, no chips, and not stained or heavily crazed.

2. Well Modelled.

Early from the mould, with sharp facial details and features.

3. Well Coloured.

The enamels will not be flaked or faded, and preferably with under glaze blue or black.

Titled.

This applies mainly to Portrait figures; a titled version of a figure will always be more desirable than an untitled one.

Apart from the above points, there are two other important factors, **RARITY** and **DESIRABILITY**. When figures meet all these criteria, record prices are paid.

Rarity and Desirability

There are many figures where only a few examples are known; therefore, if the figure is desirable, the price will be affected, as the number of collectors wanting the figure will exceed the number of figures available.

Whatever the reason for a figure to be desirable – from a collector choosing a theme which interests them to a person collecting dogs of a certain breed – there are many reasons why some figures are much more desirable than others. The list might seem endless, but as a general rule if it is desirable to you for one reason, there is always another reason why it is desirable to someone else.

Coloured Versus White

In today's market a coloured figure will always be more expensive than its white counterpart. White figures at the time of production were not necessarily any less expensive, as they often have a large amount of gilding, which would have required a further firing and subsequent burnishing.

These figures should not be confused with the figures made towards the decline of production. After circa 1875 figures on the whole are usually poorly coloured and moulded and painted with 'bright gold', which made a further firing unnecessary.

The occurrence of 'bright gold' is a good guide for dating a figure; figures before circa 1875 have 'best gold', which is a realistic gilding, whereas 'bright gold' is harsh and brassy in appearance.

Where is the Best Place to Purchase Your Figures?

Specialist Dealers

Although we have a vested interest, we believe that the best place to purchase figures is from a specialist dealer. They will have a large selection to choose from, the figures may be handled, and you will be able to obtain advice and information on each figure.

Any repair or restoration will be pointed out to you, and many will be happy to part-exchange or buy back any unwanted figures. You will not be sold reproductions and the dealer will usually seek out particular figures for you.

Higher prices are being paid at auction for figures than they would have if the figures had been bought from specialist dealers. The reason for this is that with the introduction of Thesaurus, The Internet (online auctions), and auction houses targeting collectors (telephone bids are now common), private collectors are bidding against **each other** to a level that dealers will not go.

Fairs and Markets

If you are looking for a bargain or just hoping to come across an unexpected find, the best places to search are street markets and fairs. Dealers will usually arrive early, so it is advisable to be there when they go in.

There are now major antique fairs in both the United Kingdom and the United States, where there will be an array of dealers selling a whole spectrum of antiques, and it is not uncommon to even find a Staffordshire exhibitor.

Auction Houses

Many of the auction houses now regularly hold specialist Staffordshire sales. Be careful at auctions, very often the condition is not stated and a repair or restoration can be missed. Ask for a condition report, and try to thoroughly examine the figure. Once the hammer has dropped, it is yours; determine a price before the sale and stick to it.

Where is the Best Place to Sell Your Figures

If you are selling, whether it is one figure or a whole collection, there are two main ways of selling your figures: -

A Dealer

The dealer should give you a fair price and pay it to you straight away.

An Auction House

If you decide to put your figures into auction, make sure that you are allowed to put realistic reserves on the figures. Insist that the figures are put in a specialist and not general sale. Be ready to wait for payment, although there are regular specialist sales, they are not that frequent, so it could at worse take up to six months from the time you submit your figures till payment.

Repair and Restoration

Staffordshire figures are very breakable objects. Considering that the majority were on open display, and some used as spill vases, it is not surprising that over the course of years many of them were damaged. The degree of damage will affect the price; a perfect piece will always command a premium over a damaged one.

1. A **RESTORED** figure exists when a piece of the figure, i.e. a paw, leg or head, is missing and the restorer has had to make a replacement
2. A **REPAIRED** figure exists when a piece of the figure has been broken off and been fixed back.
3. Both **RESTORED** and **REPAIRED** figures may have been repainted and re-fired.

There are of course degrees of repair and restoration, and it is more desirable to have a figure where only a small, unimportant piece has been replaced, rather than having that figure after it has been badly damaged and was once in many pieces.

There are many instances when a figure is so rare or desirable that restoration or repair has to be accepted, as the chances of finding a perfect example are near impossible. In these cases, it is surprising the amount that has to be paid for even a damaged figure.

Restorers and Restoration

Most specialist dealers will have had any damaged figures repaired or restored prior to sale, so it is when buying a figure from another source that you might need to have a figure repaired or restored.

Good restorers are difficult to find, and there are many out there with differing levels of ability. Before entrusting a restorer with your figures, ask to see examples of the restorers work in order to check their level of competence.

Ideally restoration of a figure should not take place unless the restorer has another figure to work from, or at the very least a clear, correct photograph. Figures have in the past been restored from a photograph of an incorrectly restored figure.

When having a figure restored, it is important to remember that it will cost just as much to have a £100.00 ($180) figure restored as a £1500.00 ($2700) one. At the time of writing, a repair to a relatively clean break across the neck in England will cost around £50.00 ($90). This is a substantial investment in the cheaper figure, but relatively small in the dearer one. This should be borne in mind; otherwise you may well end up with an expensive restored figure, when the same or similar perfect figure could have been purchased for less.

In our experience of the market, there are more repaired, restored, and damaged figures than there are perfect ones. A collector who refuses to have other than perfect figures is likely to have a limited collection, missing out on figures which will not come his way again

We have found that, if you see a figure that you like but it has a little bit of damage, if the price reflects the damage, the best course of action is to buy it. It is always possible to exchange it or sell it on if a better example turns up.

Reproductions and Fakes

Virtually all Staffordshire figures from 1835 to 1875 were made using the press mould method, and the resulting figures are heavier than those made by the slip mould process. During the middle part of the nineteenth century, large amounts of lead and arsenic were used in the glazing process. These ingredients were responsible for the lustrous glazes, but in the end caused the early death of the 'Dipper'. This was the man responsible for dipping the figures into the liquid glaze prior to firing, spending most of his working life with his arms submersed in this poisonous mixture.

Even in the Far East, where the majority of reproductions are now being imported from, these types of glazes are not permitted, so both the colouring and glaze of these reproductions do not compare with an original.

More and more reproductions are appearing on both the U.K. and U.S. markets. They were previously very easy to identify as most were made using slip moulds, which made them lighter. The more recent reproductions produced in the Far East have been using the origi-

nal press mould method, giving them the weight and feel of their contemporary counterparts. But the colouring and glaze still does not compare with the originals.

The Difference Between Press and Slip Moulds Are: -

A PRESS MOULD – A bat of clay, like a pancake, is pressed by hand into the mould. This mould is usually in three parts or more depending on the complexity of the figure being produced. A three-part mould consists of the front, the back, and the bottom. The excess clay is then trimmed off, the whole bound together, and fired.

A SLIP MOULD – The mould is preformed and hollow, and the slip (a clay that has a consistency of cream) is poured into the mould, and then left to dry, any excess being poured out prior to firing.

Recognising Reproduction

One of the most difficult things for the new or inexperienced collector is to tell the genuine from the reproduction. This is something that cannot be learnt quickly, it can take many years to be totally sure about every figure they might come by.

Once again, this is where specialist dealers can help; they will be able to give you pointers, and you will be able to see a lot of genuine Staffordshire together. Handling Staffordshire is the only way to really learn; an early Victorian Staffordshire figure should have been made from a press mould, have a good weight to it, an uneven glaze, and vibrant colour. If it seems light, suspect it.

To Identify a Reproduction

Look carefully at the glaze, a lead glaze tends to be deep, rich, and uneven; modern glazes tend to be thin, smooth, and very even. Look carefully at the colouring; underglaze blue is particularly difficult to reproduce convincingly. Colours on reproduction figures tend to be brighter, and not so subdued. Also, many of the reproductions use colours which were never originally used.

If a figure has been made from a slip mould, features such as the nose are smooth rather than pointed, and the features are painted on and not moulded in the figure.

Original figures are decorated, that is the colours are delicately applied, often with 'combing'. Great care was often taken, employing hundreds of small brush strokes. Reproductions are generally 'coated' with paint, having very little or no decoration.

Do not be convinced a figure is old because the glaze is cracked; this craquelure is easy to reproduce and is not necessarily a sign of age.

Fakes

Fakes in Staffordshire are rare, for the market is now cluttered with reproductions to deceive the unwary. To manufacture a fake would take a considerable amount of time and trouble, and any person trying to fake a figure would find it difficult to fool the experts, dealers, and auction houses, who are sufficiently knowledgeable to recognise a figure that has been tampered with.

The most common faking and the easiest to accomplish is the adding of a title to an untitled figure, but this does not really apply to dog figures and groups. In 1998, the faking of dogs with baskets in their mouths occurred. The price of these figures has escalated in the past few years and it seems that a faker realised a profitable market. The dogs themselves are original, but what is happening is that baskets are being applied carefully to their mouths. As a general rule the best course of action is to look very carefully at their mouths and baskets, look for over painting and any join marks.

There has also appeared on the market a pair of dog groups that are very convincing. We did include these in *Book Two* under Fig. Nos. 2696/2697. A detailed examination leads us to believe that they are not Staffordshire and were probably made in France, a derivation of this pair can also be found where, instead of a group, just the single dogs are modelled.

Very recently another pair of dogs have been 'reproduced', but to a standard that they must be considered fakes. Pairs of Figures 2554/2555 of a spaniel and pup on a blue base have been turning up in auction rooms and at fairs. On the examples that the author has seen, the dog is black and the pup is red, but this could change. They are very convincing and have fooled a number of auction houses and great care should be taken when purchasing these figures.

Misattributions and the Identification of Figures

It is in the field of misattributions that the greatest care should be taken. Over the years many figures have, on little if no evidence, been attributed to a particular person or production. Dealers have not always done this with a profit in mind.

The majority of Staffordshire figures were modelled and made with no particular person in mind. The hundreds of decorative figures are just that, decorative; their purpose for a mass market was to brighten up a shelf or mantelpiece.

The difference in price has caused many of the figures of children with dogs to be passed off as 'The Royal Children'. Many figures are said to be of actors or actresses in specific roles and it is possible that a proportion of them are, but unless there is definite proof (i.e., a music front [sheet music], engraving, etc.,), care should be taken.

A number of the earliest collectors were actors or others connected to or with a love of the theatre, and we have them to thank for some of the attributions that we have today. They spent many hours trawling through early music fronts, playbills, and prints. Though, in some cases, over enthusiasm has led to decorative figures being given erroneous theatrical attributions.

While the potter's titled the Queen, who would have been identifiable to nearly all of her subjects, they rarely titled actors, even though the actor would have been identifiable to very few. The reason they did not is that they were portraying, at best, the dramatic moment and the actor was of little consequence.

The Parr factory produced a number of figures based on engravings from Tallis's 'Shakespeare Gallery'. These figures were all titled with the character or play, the engravings all had details of the actor or actress portraying the parts, but the figures are never, with one exception, found titled with the names of the actor or actress. They were unimportant, for it was the dramatic moment that was being portrayed.

History

The county of Staffordshire has been producing pottery of all types for many years. The area in which the majority of it was produced was geographically quite small, made up of seven villages covering a mere thirty square miles. What these villages had in common was an abundance of coal to fuel the kilns and a more than a sufficient supply of clay to make the figures.

These seven villages of Stoke, Fenton, Longton, Tunstall, Burslem, Hanley, and Shelton grew into towns and finally into The County Borough of Stoke on Trent. The scale of production of pottery and porcelain in these towns was immense, for it was not just figures that were produced, but every conceivable item, from candlesnuffers to lavatory pans, from jardinières to dinner services. It is likely that even today each home in Great Britain possesses at least one article of domestic or decorative ware that was produced in the potteries.

Decorative, animal, and religious figures have been produced in Staffordshire since the early 1700s; this book concentrates on the specific type of design of figures known as Victorian Staffordshire. There was of course an overlapping period during which both pre-Victorian and Victorian figures were made. Attributed to one Obadiah Sherratt, who was born in about 1775, is a whole host of figures. In particular, Sherratt produced figures with 'Table bases', having either four or six feet, with titles such as 'Ale Bench' and its pair 'Tee Total', depicting either a happy or unhappy family depending on whether or not alcohol was consumed. Bull baiting was avidly watched and a group of bull, dogs, and attendant was made titled 'Bull Baiting, Now Captain Lad'. Obadiah was illiterate, he had signed his wedding certificate with a cross, and thus the spelling on many of his titles was less than accurate; for instance, a spectacular figure of a standing lion with one foot on a ball is titled 'Roran Lion'.

The most sought after, and the most expensive, of Sherratt's figures are the menagerie figures. Polito's touring menagerie had visited Staffordshire in 1808, and to commemorate, a large figure was made titled 'Polito's Menagerie'. It must have been successful, for shortly thereafter an even larger, more elaborate version was made. Polito died in 1814 and he was succeeded by a Mr. Wombwell. This second version can also be found titled 'Wombwell's Menagerie. A third, even more elaborate, version was made that is only ever found titled 'Wombwell's Menagerie'.

Obadiah died in the mid- to late 1830s and was succeeded by his son, Hamlet. By the 1850s, the business was being run by Obadiah's widow, Martha. The business appears to have ceased in about 1860. None of Sherratt's figures have ever been found factory marked and most are impossible to date within ten to twenty years of manufacture. So it is possible that these pre-Victorian figures continued being manufactured up to 1860. Alternatively, perhaps the son changed his methods of production and started to make flatbacks, which would have meant changing from as many as fifty separate handmade moulds to as few as three. Other potters who were in production both before and after 1835 would either have continued with the pre-Victorian style, or changed to meet the demand for the newer, more simplified figures of the Victorian era.

This new style of figure was a simplified version of pre-Victorian figures, which had used many handmade subsidiary parts. These new figures were very simple to produce, the majority of them needing only three moulds: a front, a back, and a base. Because of the extreme heat of the glost oven, only two colours could withstand this heat and remain unchanged. The prime colour was Cobalt blue, a hallmark of the period, although used sparingly on dog figures, usually only on the base. A derivative black or purple could also be produced, but this was rarely used.

The other colours seen on figures were added after and refired at a lower temperature. These colours are overglaze enamels. Whilst these overglaze enamels can flake, the blue and black cannot. The darker the colour, the more likely is to flake. Overglaze black, that was used much more frequently than underglaze black, is the most likely to suffer.

There were numerous pot banks at this time in Staffordshire, some employing many hundreds of people, others working on a much smaller scale. This was the early part of the Victorian era, when there were no real worker's rights or effective trade unions. Workers were employed in near slave labour conditions. Children as young as five years of age were expected to work twelve hours a day, six days a week. They were used for the menial tasks, carrying the clay, pressing the moulds, and painting and decorating the figures.

When and which pot bank produced the first 'flatback' will never be known, but what is certain is that it did not take other potteries too long to realise the commercial value of this style of figure. It would be inaccurate to suggest that styles of production changed on a particular date at the beginning of the Victorian period; it is more than probable that the early style of figure carried on in tandem with the 'flatbacks' for a number of years. The ease and cheapness of producing these figures would have eventually forced the demise of the earlier hand modelled figures.

There were exceptions to this, and even though the style of the figure changed, a few potteries did continue to produce figures in the round. These figures had moved on from their pre-Victorian counterparts, having the look and feel of Victorian Staffordshire, the difference being that they were still modelled and decorated all round. The perceived wisdom has been that the Parr factory produced the majority of these figures, although during recent excavations of the Dudson factory site, a number of shards found were similar to figures at present described as Parr figures.

To the majority of collectors of Staffordshire figures, which pottery produced which figure is unimportant, probably due to the fact that the vast majority of figures are unmarked. Refreshingly, Staffordshire figure collectors are not afflicted by the need to have a mark or a stamp on the bottom of a figure, a condition suffered by so many collectors of other pottery and porcelain. The bottom of a figure is usually the last place a collector or a dealer will look when deciding whether or not to buy a Victorian Staffordshire figure.

The legacy left by the Victorian potters are the wonderful figures we have today. For about forty years a standard was maintained. After that time, with a few exceptions, debased, cheaper versions appeared, decorating ended, and – if the figures were coloured at all – they were coated rather than decorated. The best gold that had been used for the gilding was abandoned and a bright, brassy, cheaper method applied. The production continued but the heyday was over and the quality was never to be seen again.

The Makers and the Modellers.

The Modellers

The true Staffordshire artist was not the factory that produced the figures, but the modeller who made the original and produced the first moulds. There were a large number of small pot banks. It would have not been economically viable for each and every factory to employ their own full time modeller, and for the small family pot banks it would have been impossible. So, unless that talent existed within the family, they would have to buy models. So it would be to the travelling, self-employed modeller that these pot banks would go for their figures.

We have no documented evidence to prove this, but there is evidence in the form of signed work. In the Pugh collection, housed at The City Museum and Art Gallery, Hanley, Stoke-on-Trent, there is a finely modelled figure of Admiral Sir Charles Napier, the base of which is inscribed 'John Carr 1857'. No records of any factory bearing this name are recorded in Staffordshire, and the figure is not a product of the Parr factory, so we must assume this is a signature of the artist himself.

Plate 1 illustrates this point. These whippets are products of the Parr factory, bearing all the recognised hallmarks, and the bases are inscribed 'J. C. Hanley June 30 1854' and the writing is similar to the hand of the Napier figure. This would seem to prove that one modeller has been identified, who had worked for at least two different factories. As Mr. John Carr signed two of his works, it is likely that he has signed more, as he was working at the height of production. It will be interesting to see whether any more of his work is discovered.

It would appear from the above that not only did the modeller design the figure, but that he would have also overseen the first stages of production, signing his pieces prior to firing. Only the very first figures would have been signed, and this would explain their rarity.

With the above exception, we are unable to attribute figures to a particular modeller, and indeed their names remain obscure. Mr. Haggar, in his 1955 book *Staffordshire Chimney Ornaments*, said that he had been told by an old pottery printer that Sampson Smith's figures were modelled by 'Edwards of East Vale' but that he had been unable to discover any modeller of that name. He also said that the unusual pseudo-baroque figures, which were made by Sampson Smith, were the work of a Giovanni Meli, a Sicilian trade modeller who worked in Rome Street, Stoke, from about 1845 until 1865. He did not, however, attribute any particular figure to Mr. Meli.

Mr. Haggar's book, in his appendix, lists over twenty modellers who worked at the relevant times. Even after this publication of nearly fifty years ago, figures have still not been able to be attributed to named modellers and it is extremely unlikely now that they ever will be.

PLATE 1/2
Illustrated are a pair of seated Whippets with hares, and the base of one of these figures is inscribed, J. C. Hanley June 30 1854.

The Makers

Unlike the modellers, there is some documentary evidence as to which factory made figures, and in some instances particular figures can be attributed to a particular potter. What is surprising is that Minton's, which was by far the largest employer with over 1500 people employed and for which records survive, has no evidence that they produced flatbacks. The same can also be said of another major potter and employer, Wedgwood. Doulton of Lambeth did produce a pair of figures of Albert and Victoria that were titled, but these were in stoneware and they did not move to the potteries until 1877. It was not until then that they diversified into earthenware, and their products from that date are well documented and not at all flatbacks. So, if the major potters did not, then who did?

James Dudson

This pottery was one of the few that worked throughout the Victorian period, their factory was in Hope & Hanover Streets, Hanley and was operational from 1838 until 1888. It continued as J.T. Dudson from 1888 until 1898 and then changed its name to Dudson Bros (Ltd.) and has continued ever since.

They advertised that they made 'Earthenware's, Figures etc.' Most of their marked work is of jasper ware in the Wedgwood style.

Relatively recent excavations at the factory have turned up shards, which in a number of respects are similar to figures believed to have been made at The Parr-Kent factory. Fig. 3321C, a tobacco jar in the form of a Turks head is marked on the base 'DUDSON' and Figure. 2834, a parrot perched on a tree stump, has been identified by Miss A. Dudson as having been made in the Dudson factory. As this factory produced wares for the whole of the period, there must be many more yet to be identified figures that were made there.

John & Rebecca Lloyd

This partnership commenced in 1834 and continued until 1852. It is believed that John Lloyd died in 1850 and that his wife Rebecca continued for two years after his death. The pottery was at Shelton, Hanley. Unlike most of the Staffordshire potters, they did factory mark some of their figures, in particular a pair of figures of Victoria with a baby and Albert can be found marked 'LLOYD SHELTON'. Many of their figures are more porcelain than pottery. They continued to model in the round with many separate moulds, a particular example being the group of Van Amburgh (see Figure 336 VSF 1835-1875, Book One). Their figures are usually of very good quality, but they do not appear to have made any 'flatbacks', probably because they ceased production before these figures were in their heyday.

The Parr-Kent Factory

This pottery commenced at 34 Church St., Burslem under the auspices of Mr. Thomas Parr in 1852. It continued under this name until 1870, when the name and address changed to Mr. John Parr at Wellington St., Burslem.

A Mr. William Kent had been in partnership with Gaskell and Parr in Burslem. This partnership was dissolved in 1878. At that time, Mr. Kent built a factory at Auckland St., Burslem and traded from that date until 1894 under the name Kent & Parr. The Kent & Parr name survived until 1894, when the pottery became William Kent. Finally, in 1944 it became William Kent (Porcelains) Ltd. Production of figures ceased at the end of 1962.

As late as 1955, William Kent issued a coloured catalogue of their range of figures. Many of these can be identified as having first been produced in the 1850s to 1860s. It is certain that a number of the figures in the catalogue were not originally made by The Parr-Kent factory, for as other potteries went out of business Parr-Kent acquired the moulds and continued production.

This company of potters started at the beginning of production of Victorian Staffordshire and continued late into the twentieth century. They were amongst the first, and were certainly the last, to produce figures. Their range was enormous, partly due to buying other potters' moulds.

When most other potteries were making flatbacks, Parr-Kent had to a major extent ignored the mainstream and continued to make figures in the round. For whatever reason, they were successful and continued long after their competitors had ceased. Their earlier production is superior to that made later. Gradually the decoration, which in the earlier figures of the 1850s and 1860s is a delicate combing of colours – particularly on the base, becomes a coating of paint in a block of colour in the 1880s and 1890s. The modelling remains quite good throughout, and it is from the palette used that the figures can best be dated. One other minor idiosyncracy of the Parr pottery is that on many of the decorative figures of women and girls, their shoes were often painted red.

Poole & Unwin

This pottery started in 1871 at the Corn Hill Works, Longton. By , it had changed its name to Joseph Unwin & Co. A figure of two harvesters, Fig. 2019, has been recorded with two different marks. One example bears the mark 'Unwin' in a diamond on the back of the figure, the other the initials 'P & U' on the base. The figure bears some resemblance to figures known to have been made by Sampson Smith, so possibly the same modeller was used by both potteries.

Ridgway & Robey

Little is known of this partnership, as they only existed for under two years. Their works were in Hanley and the partners were William Ridgway and Ralph Mayer Robey. Their claim to fame was that they produced a series of Dickensian figures and marked them fully with 'Published June 15 1839 by Ridgway & Robey Hanley Staffordshire Potteries'. The figures are very rare and owe more to Pre-Victorian figures in their style, as they are modelled in the round, decorated back and front, and have a number of subsidiary moulds.

William Ridgway also appeared to have another factory with his son for a period of ten years from 1838 to 1848, but no figures from this Company are known.

Sampson-Smith

Sampson Smith was born in 1813 and died in 1878. He is recorded as a pottery decorator. His obituary notice described him as 'a well-known and highly respected

13

china manufacturer carrying on business in Barker St. The funeral was at St. James Church, Longton and was attended by a great throng of people. There were twenty coaches. The crowd in the churchyard was dispersed by a bull that had broken loose. Not the Bull in the proverbial china shop!

It is not known for certain when the pottery first started, but a number of figures have been recorded with a mark of either 'Sampson Smith 1851 Longton' or 'S Smith Longton 1851'. These were not the dates of the figures, so it could be safely assumed that the pottery had put the date of its inception on the figures.

Until 1859 Sampson Smith was making these figures at The Garfield Pottery, High St., Longton, and from 1859 until his death, at The Sutherland Pottery.

What makes this pottery important to Staffordshire figure history was that in 1948, in a disused part of the factory, about sixty old press moulds were discovered in good condition. This find enabled the attribution of not only the moulds found, but of many other figures that were recorded and were clearly by the same hand. Many of these related to post 1875, but a number were from the 1850s and 1860s.

Shortly after this find, a number of the moulds were put into production. Care should be taken, as the resulting figures now have fifty years of age and, either through intent or ignorance, can be passed off as nineteenth century figures.

It is also known that Sampson Smith made comforter dogs in great quantities. It is believed that they produced the dogs numbered 1 to 6, Figs. 2416 to 2427.

Many other potters of this period are known by name, and it is certain that many were producing 'Toys' or 'images', as Staffordshire figures were called. However, it has proved impossible to allocate particular figures to any of them, and after such a lapse of time it is very doubtful if it ever will.

Workers' Statements

We have written of a few of the factories that made the figures, but what of the actual people who produced them? In the early 1840s, Mr. Samuel Scriven was Her Majesty's Commissioner and was allocated the task of reporting to Parliament the condition, both moral and physical, of the children working in the potteries. He took statements from well over one hundred workers in a number of potteries. Their statements survive; they make harrowing reading, a number are here reproduced.

Earthenware Factory of Messrs Minton and Boyle, Eldon Place, Stoke, December 1840

Statement from Benjamin Taylor, Aged Twelve Years, Employed in the Press Room, Temperature in Room 98° F, in Open-air 42° F

I have worked in the press-room for 2 years; I come at half past 6 in the morning, and leave at 6 at night. I have half an hour for breakfast, 1 hour for dinner. I make cockspurs to place ware upon when it is baked; have one brother working in the same room. I get 4 shillings a week; don't know what brother gets, he is older; got a mother but no father: father has been dead 10 years; he was a presser working here he died of consumption; he was 49 when he died, I give my money to my mother; get nothing for myself; never work over hours. I go to Sunday school down to Methody's; can read, can write, can cipher a little; can tell how much 5 times 7 is, 21 and 4 times 9 is 30 (sic) my health is pretty good; can eat, drink and sleep pretty well. I find it hot in the workroom and very cold when I go out. I make no difference in clothing, summer or winter; believe there are no boys or girls in the works who do night work. I get meat for dinner three or four times a week; other day's milk and tatoes. Sometimes open the windows, but cant stand the draught

Statement from Thomas Kay, Aged Forty-six, Employed in Hot House and Throwing Room, Temperature in Room 94° F, Open-air 42° F

I have worked for Mr. Minton 18 years next Christmas. Slip making in the fore part of my service, that is making the clay for use; I now look to the ware in the hot house, besides that I beat the clay in the adjoining room; beating clay is tremendous hard work; I stand near the open door to do that, the hottest work is in the hot house, don't keep a thermometer there, heat rises from 90F to 120F tis not so hot now by a deal as in the morning we cool it now for the ware. I am paid by the quantity of work done; my average wages are about 15 shillings per week. I have a wife and 7 children, only one is a potter. I come to work at 6 in the morning sometimes 5, it depends upon what goods are in heat, leave at 3, 4, 5, and 6 and afterwards do a little job work for another master and earn 4 or 3 shillings a week. Don't find the great change of heat affects my health, it sometimes affects others, very few live to any age in such an employment, tis the hardest business of potting. I live at Harford Bridge, do not go home to dinner. I take my dinner in the throwing house get bread and cheese, no ale, but get some meat at home at night, cant read or write.

Statement from Herbert Bell, Aged Twelve, Employed in Handler's Room (looks very pale and phthisical) (sic), Temperature in Room 62° F, in Open-air 44° F

I have worked in this room 4 years as handle presser; I come at 6 and leave at 6 in the evening, I live about a mile off, I do not go home to breakfast, I go home to dinner, am allowed half an hour for breakfast and 1 hour for dinner, I work in the same room as my father, father gets so much a week piece making, does not know what father earns, all I get goes to him and mother, have a mother and sister, one works at the china works. I get no holidays, remember now, that I get about five weeks in a year, a week at Martilmas, 2 weeks in August and 1 at Whitsuntide, all the other boys get the same and a day at Christmas. I get meat at home and have clothes enough; I get a strapping sometimes; think I deserve it; father is good to me; have got a cough, have had it 3 or 4 years; feel it more in winter; I do not think the jumping on the moulds hurts me; feel no pain from it; I do not like it; I want to go into another room; I like potting would rather be a potter than a tailor or shoemaker; I never do night work. Master and overseer are very good to me, they never beat me.

Statement from George Burton, Aged Nine, Employed in the Oven, Temperature 96° F, Open-air 42° F

I work in the oven as a stoker, and carry coal to the fires; begin work at 6 o'clock and leave at 5; I do not attend at night; the oven man Henry Reach, does that from 9 o'clock at night to 5 in the morning: he then goes home, and comes again at 9, and remains all day till 5 again. He's the fireman; there are six as takes it in turn, so that one man only sits up two nights a week. His father does the same work as him. I don't know how much wages I get a week; all goes to father; he sometimes gives me a penny, sometimes two pence. I cant read, cant write. I went to Sunday school don't go now; there is no school belonging to the works, I am in good health, I have a good appetite; I get bread and cheese for dinner, sometimes tatoes and bacon; never get ale. I feel the cold on coming out of the oven; tis very hot in there, I get very thirsty there. This is all the clothes I got; I have no change at home for Sunday. Overseer very kind to me so is master. I never get a strapping, except from father sometimes.

Statement from William Hell, Aged Thirteen, Employed in the Oven Room, Temperature 100° F, Open-air 42° F

I have worked for Messrs. Minton and Boyle 2 years, first at the other bank where I ran moulds, then came here and worked in the dipping house for better than 12 months; I received there 1s. 6d per week; was never ill from that work, but some of the boys were, and one of the dippers. I left that work to work in the oven, where I am now and get 2s per week. I come about 6 in the morning, and leave about 3, because we than have nothing else to do. I find it pretty hot in the oven; we bake the ware there after it is printed. I feel the cold very much when I leave work and go home. Samuel Jones is the man who works with me; he is very good to me, never scolds or straps me. I give my money to my mother, my father is a plumber, and gets often drunk, and my mother is often

in great distress, she has 10 of us to support; 4 do no work, they are too young. Cant read; cant write; don't go to a Sunday school; never went to day school; don't know the reason why; except that mother's so poor and haven't got no clothes. I am very happy in my work, but don't get enough to eat and drink. I get mostly dry tatoes and salt; I have had no dinner today; never get meat, never get bread. Father works at Burslem, but seldom brings home any money for mother.

Statement of James Watson, Aged Forty-two, Employed in the Dipping House, Temperature 56° F, Open-air 32° F

I have been a dipper a dozen years with this firm; come at 8 leave at 4; sometimes 5 or 6. I am a fireman too and work in the gloss oven; I then sit up one night a week; as a dipper and firer I make 4s 8d per day. The nature of my employment has affected my health formerly, but has not these last two years; it is always reckoned very injurious. Three men work with me and one boy; he is 12 years of age last July and is my son; no women. There is a small portion of lead in the dipping, but it is worse elsewhere, don't think the change of heat in the ovens affects me much.

Statement of Ann Dishly, Aged Nine, Employed by Mr Joseph Clementson, High Street Shelton (Earthenware), as a Painter.

I have been a painter for 12 months last Martinmas. There are eight little girls work in the same room with me. Mary Worrelow looks after us; we all come to work at six o'clock in the morning, and go home at six, some go home to dinner, an hour is allowed us for dinner, and half an hour for breakfast. I can read very well but can't write; I go to Bethesda Sunday school and went two years to day school, they didn't teach me to write. Ann Dishly is very good to us, she never flogs us, or master either; she is my mother. We get holidays altogether perhaps a month.

Method of Production

Press Moulds

The majority of Staffordshire figures during the Victorian era were produced using press moulds, this process was as follows: -

The potter would firstly make or have made a model of the figure out of clay. Once this was done, the model would then be encased in a mould of plaster of Paris. This mould would then be divided into three parts, the front, back, and base.

Once the parts had been separated from the original model, this 'master mould' would then be placed back together, the opening filled with plaster of Paris, and then left to set.

Once set, the mould was opened, the solid figure inside would appear. This solid figure was called the 'block mould', which was kept, if other moulds were needed to be made.

The master mould was then encased in a further mould of plaster of Paris, and once set, separated into two pieces, which were then used as the working mould. The master mould was then kept in case extra working moulds were needed. It is possible that, in some cases, if a figure were for a small, limited number, then the figures would be made from the master mould.

Each of the moulds was then laid out and a flat sheet of clay, known as a 'bat', was placed on them. The clay was then pressed into the mould (it is interesting to see, quite often, on a broken figure the actual finger prints of the person who had pressed the clay into the mould). Any surplus was then trimmed off and the edges were then painted with liquid clay. The moulds were then placed together and thin rolls of clay were inserted to seal the seams inside. This was then left to dry.

Once dry, the figure was then removed from the mould and the base was applied. Any excess clay on the seams was now removed, any other moulds (i.e., separate arms, legs, etc.) applied, along with any shredded clay for decoration (i.e., ermine edged coats or foliage on the base).

A small hole was then made; this was so the air was able to escape during firing (this hole would not be necessary in the case of spill vase figures). Then the figure was placed in the kiln, receiving its first firing at around 1100C. (2000F.).

The figure now emerged in 'biscuit' form. Underglaze blue, if used, would now be painted on with fat oil and hardened by a further firing at 600C. (1100F.) to 700C. (1300F.). This was done as underglaze colour was very expensive and, without this further firing, the colour was likely to come off when dipped in the glaze.

The figure would then be 'dipped' into a liquid glaze, always containing lead, often arsenic (such glazes causing the early death of the 'dipper'), and refired in the 'glost' oven at about 950C. (1750F.).

The figure now emerged from the kiln glazed with the blue firmly fixed under the glaze and was painted with enamel (overglaze) colours and any gilding required. For the last time, the figure was fired in the kiln at between 750C. to 850C. At this heat, the enamel colours, which had been mixed with a flux that vitrifies at a lower temperature, would fuse with the previous glaze.

When the figure now came from the kiln, all that was required was the burnishing of the gilding, usually with an agate stone, and the figure was complete.

Not more than three figures a day could be made from one mould, depending on the detail of the figure they were making, and how many hours the factory worked. There could have been many working moulds of the same figure, all being made at the same time.

Due to the deposits the clay would leave in the mould, the average mould's life would not last for more than 100 figures without severe loss of quality. This may be observed by looking at individual figures. The cleaner and crisper the details on a figure, the earlier it was produced in the moulds life. The more often the mould was used, the less the quality of the figure produced.

Slip Moulds

The process of constructing a slip mould is very similar to that of a press mould, the only difference being that instead of pressing the clay in to the mould, the mould was put together and a liquid clay known as 'slip' was poured into it. This was then left for up to half an hour and the residue was then poured out. The remainder was left to dry. When dry, it was taken from the mould and the base was applied in the same manner as the press mould, although it was not always common practice to apply a base.

The use of slip moulds was not popular, not because of the process, which if anything was less time consuming, but because a slip mould would deteriorate much quicker. The slip mould had to be replaced after as little as twenty figures, whereas a press mould could easily produce five times as many.

In practice, virtually NONE of the early Victorian Staffordshire figures were made by slip moulds, although quite a few of the later figures (after 1875) were made by this method.

The Use of Colour in Staffordshire Figures

The use of colour in Staffordshire figures was at its height from the 1840s to 1860s. After this period the use of colour gradually declined until little if any was used. The most vibrant colours on Staffordshire figures were underglaze blue and black. These colours, as the name suggests, were under the glaze, so even now they are as stunning as the day when they came out of the factory. The other colours that were used were enamels, which were on top of the glaze (even though they had been re-fired in the kiln), so are prone to flaking and discolouring over a period of time. Over glaze black, which is the darkest of all the colours, is the most likely to flake. The darker the enamel colour, the more flaking is likely to occur.

Both coloured and white versions of the same figure were made at the same time, as there was a market for both types of figure.

The Use of Gold in Decoration and Titling

During the production of Victorian Staffordshire figures, two types of gilding have been used, and this has now become another useful tool for dating figures. Up until about 1875 'Best gold' was used. This was a mixture of real gold and mercury, applied to the figures before the final firing. This application of 'Best gold' was a time consuming process, as when it came out of the kiln, the gold was flat and required burnishing.

The other type of gilding, used from circa 1875 onwards, was 'Bright gold'. Bright gold was painted on and did not need firing or burnishing afterwards. Although a quicker process, it has a brassy, harsh appearance when compared to 'Best gold', which was more subdued, more gold than brass. Bright gold was not as permanent as 'Best gold' and has not withstood the test of time. Often figures that were decorated with 'Bright gold' are now found with most of it missing.

The use of titling on figures varies, but it was very seldom used on dog groups. It is interesting to note that there are different methods of titling. It is not known whether different potters preferred different titling. It is also unknown why the same figure can be found titled or untitled. The only logical explanation can be cost, as the application of gold required extra work. It is not uncommon to find a figure decorated in gold, but the title has been omitted, no reason for this has been found. One theory is that they might have been intended to sell not as a portrait, but as a decorative figure.

The different types of titling that can be found are listed below: —

RAISED BLACK CAPITALS – These seem to appear rarely on figures, but when they do, they are normally complemented by use of best gold, thus confirming they were not used for cheapness, as they would have required burnishing afterwards.

BLACK TRANSFERS – These are also rarely used, but do tend to be used when a lot of script is involved, i.e., quoting large amounts of text.

RAISED GILT CAPITALS – One of the more common ways of titling: In the Victorian era illiteracy was common, particularly amongst the working class, so this method needed little skill to apply, and mistakes could be avoided.

GILT SCRIPT – A form of titling that would require a degree of literacy, although it is possible that the artist was able to copy the name 'Prince' or 'Princess' but not write his or her own.

INDENTED CAPITALS – This type of titling was used by a small number of potteries. One such firm was the Parr factory, which used black indents in titling its figures. Another pottery using gilt indents, of which less is known, is referred to as the 'Alpha' factory, but this pottery was probably a modeller and not a factory. This process would not have been done in the mould, but would have to have been applied quite quickly after a piece had been removed and prior to its first firing.

Types of Nineteenth Century Staffordshire Figures

By 1875, most of the figures that were being produced had little or no colour at all, and the gold decoration was painted on, giving the figures a harsh, brassy look. Little care seems to have been taken in the original model, and consequently the figures themselves were of little quality. There were exceptions to this, and the Parr factory continued to maintain a standard, although not up to the quality of their earlier work. Perhaps, with hindsight, it would have been best for the potters to stop production at this point, but they did not, carrying on producing figures of ever decreasing quality for the next thirty years.

What was Potted?

The subjects chosen by the potters were as varied as the times in which they lived; but, the sole overriding reason for their production was for a profit. Each and every pottery, no matter how small, had to be profitable to survive. Artistic merit was hardy contemplated. Above and beyond every other consideration, the figure had to sell. A number of the figures produced did not sell. Today that would make them rare, if they are of quality, as well as being rare. They are now highly regarded and consequently will be expensive.

Chapter One
Dogs

The dog has had a relationship with man from time immemorial, a relationship which no other animal has or is ever likely to have. It is, and has been, a guard, protector, companion, servant, and friend. From its origins as a wolf, it has been bred to such a variety, that it is now very difficult to believe that such dogs as the Mexican Hairless and the Great Dane could have the same ancestor.

The dog continues to serve man in many roles, as a retriever in the field, a terrier to eliminate rats, a hound to destroy foxes, a finder of drugs, a policeman's assistant, and now it has been found that some dogs are able to detect cancer cells in man by their smell. It has now insinuated itself so far into the human psyche that, for some, they would sooner lose their wife or husband than their dog!

It is the Spaniel dog that most people view as typical Staffordshire. They were known in England as Comforters, and in Scotland as Wally Dugs. They sat on either side of the mantelpiece and viewed the world with unconcern. Their origin or inspiration is thought to be the pet King Charles Spaniel 'Dash' that was kept by Queen Victoria, that she had owned since she was a young girl. When she became Queen, Dash was her constant companion and became well known, he himself being the subject of many prints and wool work pictures. There is not however any figure of her with Dash recorded.

The first Comforters appeared at the beginning of the 1840s and they continued to be made well into the 1900s. By the 1880s, like most Staffordshire, the quality of the figures had deteriorated and the bulk of the production consisted of white, badly modelled dogs decorated in bright gold, the previously painted eyes replaced in many instances with glass ones.

The potters, realising that they were onto a commercial success, produced these animals in amazing variety, quantity, and in many sizes. They did not restrict their production to spaniels, producing figures of many other breeds. One of the most popular of these breeds was the Whippet, a small Greyhound, kept by many in rural areas. Let loose on the land, Whippets were able to catch rabbits for the pot, the dog being able to venture where the owner might either be shot or fall foul of a man trap. Not only were King Charles Spaniels potted, but also a whole range of breeds, from Whippets to Bull Mastiff's, Poodles to St. Bernard's.

Amongst the rarities made were pairs of gun dogs and today these are amongst the most sought after figures, and consequently the most expensive. But none are so popular as the spaniel and Whippet, which appear in this chapter. We have, where possible, identified the breed, but many defy identification, as some were not pure bred.

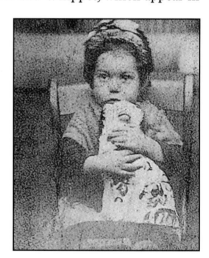

A contemporary photograph of a young girl in a pushchair holding a comforter spaniel. The caption beneath reads "Bertha Ellen Green with her doggie."

This Chapter is Divided into the Following Sections:

The two most prolific models, spaniels and Whippets, are listed first, followed by an alphabetical listing of the rest:

i. Spaniels 19
ii. Whippets 76
iii. Alsatian 92
iv. Bull Mastiffs 92
v. Dalmatians 93

vi. Game Dogs 95
vii. Pekinese.................................... 110
viii. Poodles 112
ix. Pugs & Bulldogs 121
x. Unidentified Breeds 126

i. Spaniels

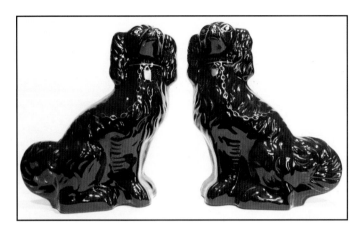

Figs. Size 1, 2416/2417, Size 2, 2418/2419, Size 3, 2420/2421, Size 4, 2422/2423, Size 5, 2424/2425, Size 6, 2426/2427

The typical Comforter, one factory in particular made them in six sizes, and on the bottom impressed the size number 1, being the largest, and 6, being the smallest. The size 1 is different from the others in so far as instead of the tail curling around in front, it curls up and around to the side. The only other difference is that sizes 2 and 3 have chains across their bodies which sizes 4, 5, and 6 do not.

It is improbable that they were sold in sets, and any set now in existence has likely been assembled, they have been photographed as a group as to show them separately would not show the size differential. The most popular was the red and white, but these dogs can also be found in black and white, lustre and white, white, with or without gilding, and in underglaze black.

A pair of Size 1, illustrated in underglaze black.

The smallest size 6 is by far the most difficult pair to find.

There is also illustrated pair of size 2's. These dogs have black muzzles and black trimmed paws. They are not found with an impressed number on the base. Apart from this, they are almost identical to the numbered series. These can also be found in six sizes.

They were no doubt the product of another competing potter.

HEIGHT: **Size 1, 2416/2417, 13 inches; Size 2, 2418/2419, 10 inches; Size 3, 2420/2421, 9 inches; Size 4, 2422/2423, 7.75 inches; Size 5, 2424/2425, 6.5 inches; Size 6, 2426/2427, 5.5 inches**

PRICE: Pair: D, Singles: F; For the set of six pairs: A+ (Prices are for red and whites, for others the price will be less.)

Fig. 2417A
A seated spaniel with collar, locket, and chain. An unusual example, it is almost identical to Fig 2417, but is smaller and has an oblong round cornered base. **There is a pair to this and figure 2416A has been reserved for it.**
HEIGHT: 10 inches
PRICE: Pair E Singles F

Figs. 2428/2429
A pair of white spaniels with gilded collars and grey paws. **Theses figures can be found in two sizes, both illustrated.**
HEIGHT: 9.25 inches, 7.25 inches
PRICE: Pairs: E, Singles: F

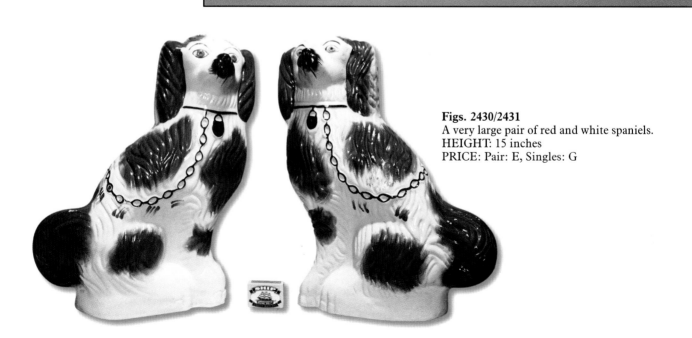

Figs. 2430/2431
A very large pair of red and white spaniels.
HEIGHT: 15 inches
PRICE: Pair: E, Singles: G

Figs. 2432/2433
A pair of white and gilt seated spaniels. As with many of the spaniel pairs, examples can be found in red and white, black and white, white and gilt, and lustre. Two pairs are illustrated, identical dogs, one pair decorated in black and white, the others in white and gilt.
HEIGHT: 9.5 inches
PRICE: Pair: E, Singles: F

Figs. 2434/2435
A pair of white and gilt spaniels, similar to but larger than Figures 2432/2433.
HEIGHT: 11.5 inches
PRICE: Pair: F, Singles: G

Figs. 2435A/2435B
A pair of red and white seated spaniels.
These dogs are very similar to Figs. 2434/2435, with the exception that they have collars and no chain. The dogs illustrated have over the years 'flaked', the enamel red has been lost in patches. In the hands of a good restorer, they can very easily be returned to their original condition.
HEIGHT: 11 inches
PRICE: Pair: E, Singles: F.

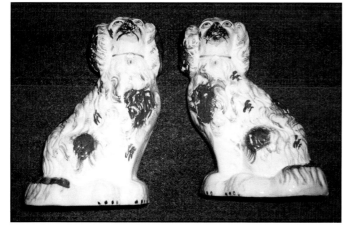

Figs. 2436/2437
A large pair of red and white spaniels, very finely modelled and delicately painted.
HEIGHT: 14 inches
PRICE: Pair: D, Singles: F

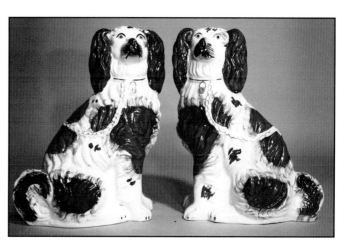

Figs. 2438/2439
A pair of white and gilt spaniels. These dogs are decorated in 'bright' or late gold, and would not have been made before 1870 and quite possibly later, however they are very well modelled and the gilt is in unusually pristine condition.
HEIGHT: 11 inches
PRICE: Pair: E, Singles: G

Figs. 2440/2441
A pair of red and white spaniels.
HEIGHT: 8.5 inches
PRICE: Pair: E, Singles: G

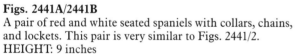

Figs. 2441A/2441B
A pair of red and white seated spaniels with collars, chains, and lockets. This pair is very similar to Figs. 2441/2.
HEIGHT: 9 inches
PRICE: Pair: E, Singles: F.

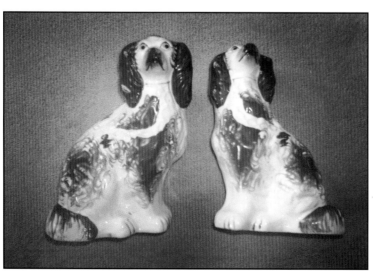

Figs. 2441C/2441D
A pair of red and white, seated spaniels with collars and chains.
HEIGHT: 6.5 inches
PRICE: Pair: E, Singles: F.

It is not known how many potters made comforter dogs. It would be surprising if a particular potter made a number of versions that differed slightly. It is probable that different potters were responsible for the enormous number of variants that are to be found. Pairs differ in size, decoration, and colouring as well as being modelled with and without chains and lockets. Examples can be found with tails curled to the side, erect or in front. That is why the prospect of finding a matching pair, should one have been lost, is so difficult.

Figs. 2446/2447
A pair of red and white spaniels.
HEIGHT: 7.5 inches
PRICE: Pair: F, Singles: G

Figs. 2442/2443
A pair of red and white spaniels.
HEIGHT: 8 inches
PRICE: Pair: E, Singles: F

Figs. 2447A/2447B
A pair of red and white seated spaniels with collars and lockets
HEIGHT: 6.75
PRICE: Pair: E, Single: F.

Figs. 2444/2445
A pair of red and white spaniels.
HEIGHT: 8 inches
PRICE: Pair: E, Singles: F

Figs. 2448/2449
A pair of red and white seated spaniels, with collars and lockets. These figures and others like them can also be found decorated as 'Disraeli' spaniels.
HEIGHT: 10 inches
PRICE: Pair: F, Singles: G.

23

Figs. 2450/2451
A pair of red and white seated spaniels
with collars and lockets.
HEIGHT: 8.5 inches
PRICE: Pair: E, Singles: G.

Figs. 2452/2453
A pair of red and white seated spaniels
with lockets.
HEIGHT: 7 inches
PRICE: Pair: F, Singles: G.

Figs. 2454/2455
A large pair of red and white seated
spaniels with lockets and chains.
HEIGHT: 12.5 inches
PRICE: Pair: E, Singles: G.

Figs. 2456/2457
A pair of red and white spaniels with
lustre collars and black chains.
HEIGHT: 8.5 inches
PRICE: Pair: F, Singles: G.

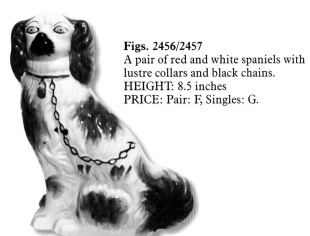

Figs. 2458/2459
A pair of red and white seated
spaniels with lockets and chains.
HEIGHT: 11 inches
PRICE: Pair: E, Singles: F.

Figs 2460/2461
A pair of red and white spaniels with
lockets.
This figure can be found in two sizes,
4.75 inch version illustrated.
HEIGHT: 6 inches, 4.75 inches
PRICE: Pair: G, Singles: H.

Figs. 2462/2463
A pair of red and white seated spaniels with lockets.
HEIGHT: 4 inches
PRICE: Pair: G, Singles: H.

Figs. 2466/2467
A pair of seated 'chunky' red and white spaniels with collars,
chains, and lockets.
HEIGHT: 10.75 inches
PRICE: Pair: D, Singles: F.

Figs. 2464/2465
A pair of red and white seated spaniels with lockets.
Figure 2464 not illustrated.
HEIGHT: 4.5 inches
PRICE: Pair: G, Singles: H.

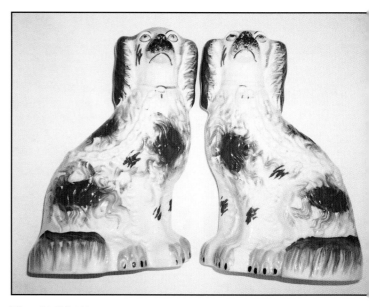

Figs. 2468/2469
A pair of red and white spaniels with locket and chain.
HEIGHT: 9.75 inches
PRICE: Pair: E, Singles: F.

Figs. 2469A/2469B
A pair of chunky red and white spaniels.
These figures are similar to Figures 2472/2473, apart from the fact they do not have separately moulded front legs. They may be found with or without a chain. Also illustrated is a single white and gilt version, titled 'EDWARD HARRISON'. When 'Titled' figures such as this are found, it confirms that the 'Title' is the name of the person to whom the figure was given. It is not the name of the figure.
HEIGHT: 12.5 inches
PRICE: Pair: D, Singles: E.

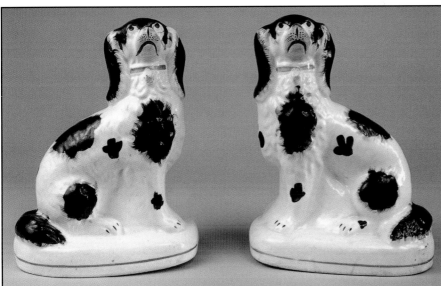

Figs. 2469C/2469D
A pair of black and white spaniels on oval gilt lined bases.
HEIGHT: 7.75 inches
PRICE: Pair: E, Singles: F.

Figs. 2469E/2469F
A pair of red and white spaniels with lockets and chains.
These figures are very finely modelled and decorated.
HEIGHT: 10.5 inches
PRICE: Pair: D, Singles: F.

The following versions, unlike Figures 2416-2469F, have more complex moulds, thus taking the potters longer to design and produce. The time taken in this process can now be appreciated, as these figures represent some of the finest spaniels to have been made. As with their simpler counterparts, these dogs may also be found in the same range of colours, although underglaze black is not generally used.

Figs. 2470/2471
A superb pair of underglaze black and white spaniels, with separately moulded front leg. These very rare dogs can also be found in red and white, underglaze, black luster, and white and gilt. They are amongst the largest and finest examples of Staffordshire comforters.
HEIGHT: 15 inches
PRICE: Pair: B, Singles: C.

Figs. 2471A/2471B
A superb pair of chunky red and white spaniels, with collars, lockets, and separately moulded front legs.
HEIGHT: 12.5 inches
PRICE: Pair: C, Singles: E.

Figs. 2472/2473
A superb pair of chunky black and white spaniels, with collars, lockets, and separately moulded front legs.
HEIGHT: 12.5 inches
PRICE: Pair: C, Singles: F.

Figs. 2473A/2473B
A pair of red and white spaniels with collars, lockets, chains, and separate moulded front legs.
HEIGHT: 11 inches
PRICE: Pair: D, Singles: F.

Figs. 2474/2475
A pair of red and white spaniels, with collars, lockets, chains, and separately moulded front legs.
HEIGHT: 7.75 inches
PRICE: Pair: D, Singles: F.

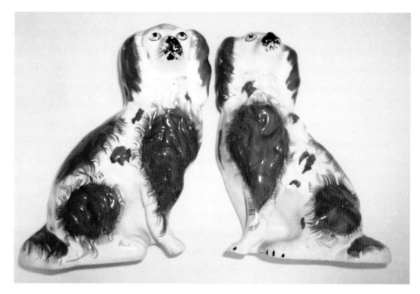

Figs. 2474A/2474B
A pair of red and white seated spaniels with a locket and separate front leg.
These figures are similar to Figs. 2474/2475, other than size and lack of chain.
HEIGHT: 6.75 inches
PRICE: Pair: E, Singles: F.

Figs. 2476/2477
A pair of red and white spaniels, with collars, locket, chains, and separately moulded front legs.
HEIGHT: 9 inches
PRICE: Pair: D, Singles: F.

Figs. 2477A/2477B
A pair of figures of red and white spaniels seated with lockets, collars, chains, and two separate front legs.
HEIGHT: 6 inches
PRICE: Pair: E, Singles: F

Figs. 2477C/2477D
A pair of figures of seated spaniels
with collars, lockets, and two
separate front legs. **These dogs are
quite late as all the colours,
including the yellow collars, are
underglaze. The red is a darker
red than that used on earlier dogs.**
HEIGHT: 7.5 inches
PRICE: Pair: F, Singles: G.

Figs. 2478/2479
A pair of red and white spaniels,
with collars, lockets, chains, and
separately moulded front legs.
HEIGHT: 9.5 inches
PRICE: Pair: D, Singles: F.

Figs. 2480/2481
A pair of red and white spaniels,
with collars, lockets, and sepa-
rately moulded front legs.
HEIGHT: 5.5 inches
PRICE: Pair: D, Singles: F.

31

Fig. 2481A
A figure of a seated spaniel with a separate leg and its coat clipped.
The figure illustrated is in the white; coloured examples can be found, which raises their price considerably. This applies to all pairs of dogs. There is a pair to this. Figure 2481B has been reserved for it.
HEIGHT: 6 inches
PRICE: Pair: F, Singles: G.

Figs. 2482/2483
A pair of red and white spaniels, with collars, lockets, and separately moulded front legs.
HEIGHT: 7.75 inches
PRICE: Pair: D, Singles, F.

Figs. 2483A/2483B
A pair of figures of seated spaniels with a separate front leg and a collar with a locket. These figure are very similar to Figs. 2482/2483. There are modelling differences, mainly in the shape of the head and tail; they are also smaller.
Right hand side figure 2483B not illustrated.
HEIGHT: 6.25 inches
PRICE: Pair: D, Singles: F.

Figs. 2484/2485
A pair of red and white spaniels, with collars, lockets, and separately moulded front legs.
HEIGHT: 9.5 inches
PRICE: Pair: F, Singles: G.

Figs. 2486/2487
A pair of white and gilt spaniels, with collars, lockets, chains, and separately moulded front legs.
The gilding on these figures is best or early gold, they were made about 1850.
HEIGHT: 12 inches
PRICE: Pair: E, Singles: G.

Figs. 2488/2489
A pair of lustre spaniels, with collars, lockets, and separately moulded front legs.
HEIGHT: 10 inches
PRICE: Pair: F, Singles: G.

Figs. 2490/2491
Two pairs of black and white spaniels with collars, lockets, and chains, differently decorated, one pair with blue eyes, both with separately moulded front legs.
These spaniels with curls on their foreheads are known as 'Disraeli' spaniels, after The Prime Minister Benjamin Disraeli, who favoured a similar hairstyle. These figures are very similar to Figs. 2486/2487 with different decoration.
HEIGHT: 10.25 inches
PRICE: Pair: D, Singles: F.

Figs. 2492/2493
A pair of black and white spaniels, with collars, lockets, chains, and separately moulded front legs.
HEIGHT: 8 inches
PRICE: Pair: F, Singles: G.

Figs. 2494/2495
A pair of black and white spaniels with collars, lockets, chains, and separately moulded front legs.
HEIGHT: 9.5 inches
PRICE: Pair: E, Singles: G.

Figs. 2495A/2495B
A pair of figures of seated spaniels, with separate front legs, collars, and lockets.
These figures are decorated all over with underglaze black. The collar and locket are in best gold and the eyes in overglaze enamel.
Most of the dogs that are completely covered in overglaze black were made after 1875 and have come to be known as 'Jackfield' dogs. The company of Craven Dunhill & Co. was in existence from 1872 until 1951. Before this they were known as Hargreaves and Craven. Their premises were in Jackfield Shropshire, so technically they were not a Staffordshire potter. They marked many of their wares with their place name 'Jackfield', hence the name became attached to the dogs. The body of clay used by them was a dark red. This type of dog subsequently was copied by many Staffordshire potters, and examples have been found marked 'Sadler'.
HEIGHT: 6.5 inches
PRICE: Pair: F, Singles: G.

Figs. 2496/2497
A pair of figures of seated spaniels with lockets, collars, chains, and two separate front legs.
These figures are early, the lustre is very fine, and the modelling extremely good. At the moment dogs decorated with gold lustre fetch much less than if they were decorated in red or black. In view of the quality of many of the early lustre dogs, this situation is unlikely to continue.
HEIGHT: 11.5 inches
PRICE: Pair: D, Singles: F.

Figs. 2498/2499
A pair of red and white spaniels with chains; they hold flower baskets in their mouths.
These dogs are very similar to Figs. 2504/2505 and are probably the same, varying only in size and minor modelling differences.
HEIGHT: 7.5 inches
PRICE: Pair: D, Singles: E.

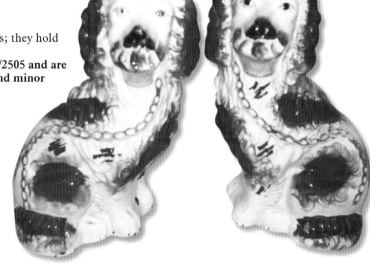

Figs. 2500/2501
A pair of red and white spaniels with baskets in their mouths.
A miniature pair, very likely made as fairings.
HEIGHT: 3.5 inches
PRICE: Pair: F, Singles: G.

Figs. 2502/2503
A pair of white and gilt spaniels, very
well modelled with flower baskets in
their mouths.
**Dogs with baskets in their mouths are
rare and eagerly sought after which
makes them expensive.**
HEIGHT: 9.5 inches
PRICE: Pair: C, Singles: E.

Figs. 2504/2505
A pair of white and gilt spaniels, with
flower baskets in their mouths.
**This pair may be found in two sizes.
The 9.5 inch version is illustrated.**
HEIGHT: 7 inches, 9.5 inches
PRICE: Pair: D, Singles: E.

Figs. 2506/2507
A pair of red and white spaniels, with
flower baskets in their mouths.
HEIGHT: 8.5 inches
PRICE: Pair: D, Singles: F.

Figs. 2508/2509
A pair of red and white spaniels, with flower baskets in their mouths.
HEIGHT: 8 inches
PRICE: Pair: D, Singles: F.

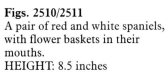

Figs. 2510/2511
A pair of red and white spaniels, with flower baskets in their mouths.
HEIGHT: 8.5 inches
PRICE: Pair: D, Singles: F.

Figs. 2511A/2511B
A pair of lustre spaniels, with flower baskets in their mouths.
It is very unusual to find flower basket dogs in lustre.
HEIGHT: 9.5 inches
PRICE: Pairs: D, Singles: F.

Figs. 2512/2513
A pair of red and white spaniels, with flower baskets in their mouths.
HEIGHT: 8 inches
PRICE: Pair: D, Singles: F.

Figs. 2514/2515
A pair of white and gilt spaniels, with flower baskets in their mouths and separate front legs.
HEIGHT: 10.5 inches
PRICE: Pair: D, Singles: F.

Figs. 2516/2517
A pair of standing red and white spaniels, with flower baskets in their mouths, Figure 2516 not illustrated.
HEIGHT: 5 inches
PRICE: Pair: F, Singles: G.

Figs. 2518/2519
A pair of seated red and white spaniels, with flower baskets in their mouths, Figure 2518 not illustrated.
HEIGHT: 6 inches
PRICE: Pair: F, Singles: G.

Figs. 2520/2521
A pair of 'Disraeli' spaniels decorated in black and white with flower baskets in their mouths.
The black enamel used on these dogs is underglaze and therefore cannot flake and they look as fresh as when they were made.
HEIGHT: 8.5 inches
PRICE: Pair: D, Singles: F.

Figs. 2522/2523
A pair of red and white recumbent spaniels.
These are very rare and were made in two sizes, the smallest are 7.75 inches in length and the largest 8.5 inches in length, they were also made with children on their backs.
HEIGHT: 6 inches
PRICE: Pair: B, Singles: E.

Figs. 2524/2525
A pair of standing red and white spaniels on arched bases decorated with leaves.
Probably the finest pair of dogs to have been produced and very rare. These dogs can be found in two sizes.
HEIGHT: 7.75 inches, 9.5 inches
PRICE: Pair: A, Singles: C.

Fig. 2525A
A spill vase figure of a recumbent spaniel with a collar and locket and a dead bird on the base. **This figure is extremely rare. Until recently Figures 2526/2527 were the only spill vase spaniels recorded. There is a pair to this figure. Figure 2525B has been reserved for it.**
HEIGHT: 7 inches
PRICE: Pair: D, Singles: E.

Figs. 2526/2527
A pair of white and gilt seated spaniels, with tree trunks to the back forming spill vases.
Early spill vase spaniel dogs are very rare. This pair is quite late. They usually have bright gold gilding, block green decoration on the base, and are rather clumpy.
HEIGHT: 13 inches
PRICE: Pair: F, Singles: G.

Fig. 2527A
A white and gilt seated spaniel, with a tree trunk to the back in the form of a spill vase.
There is a pair to this figure. Figure 2527B has been reserved for it. This figure is extremely rare, as until recently, Figures 2526/2527 were the only spill vase spaniels recorded.
HEIGHT: 13 inches
PRICE: Pair: E, Singles: G.

Fig. 2527C
A spill vase figure of a recumbent spaniel with a collar, locket, and chain and a dead bird is below.
This figure is extremely rare, as until recently, Figures 2526/2527 were the only spill vase spaniels recorded. There is a pair to this figure. Figure 2527D has been reserved for it.
HEIGHT: 8 inches
PRICE: Pair: B, Singles: D.

Figs. 2528/2529
A pair of red and white spaniels with lockets, collars, and separate front legs on a shaped base.
This pair of dogs can also be found without a base.
HEIGHT: 8 inches
PRICE: Pair: E, Singles: F.

Figs. 2530/2531
Three pairs of the same spaniels with lockets, collars, and separate front legs, each decorated differently, all of very high quality, the green bases are particularly rare.
HEIGHT: 8 inches
PRICE: Pair: D, Singles: F.

Figs. 2530A/2531A
A pair of seated black and white spaniels with lockets, collars, and separate front legs. **This pair is identical to Figures 2530/2531, other than the base has been omitted.**
HEIGHT: 6.75 inches
PRICE: Pair: E, Singles: F.

Figs. 2532/2533
A pair of red and white spaniels with lockets, collars, on cobalt blue bases, with separate front legs.
HEIGHT: 8 inches
PRICE: Pair: D, Singles: F.

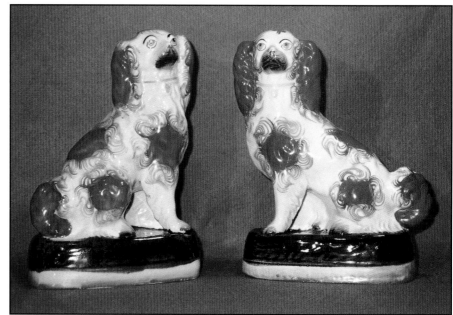

Figs. 2534A/2535A
An extremely fine pair of seated spaniels with separate front legs, collars, and lockets around their necks. **These figures are identical to Figs. 2534/2535, other than colouring and shape of the base.**
HEIGHT: 9.5 inches
PRICE: Pair: D, Singles: E.

Fig. 2535
A very finely modelled and decorated spaniel, seated on a scrolled and gilded base. There is a pair to this figure; Figure 2534 has been reserved for it.
This model has been found with the impressed mark 'LLOYD SHELTON'. It is extremely rare for Staffordshire to bear a marker's mark. John and his wife, Rebecca Shelton, were making figures from the mid-1830s until the early 1850s. This helps in the dating of this figure.
HEIGHT: 9 inches
PRICE: Pair: D, Singles: E.

Figs. 2536/2537
A pair of recumbent spaniels on fringed cushions with lockets and collars on coloured arched bases.
HEIGHT: 4.5 inches
PRICE: Pair: D, Singles: F.

Figs. 2538/2539
A pair of seated spaniels with lockets and collars on a shaped oval base.
HEIGHT: 4.5 inches
PRICE: Pair: E, Singles: G.

Figs. 2540/2541
A pair of spaniels, with lockets and collars on cobalt blue cushion bases.
HEIGHT: 4 inches
PRICE: Pair: E, Singles: G.

Figs. 2542/2543
A pair of seated spaniels with lockets, collars, and separate front legs on a shaped oval base, Figure 2543 not illustrated.
HEIGHT: 3.5 inches
PRICE: Pair: E, Singles: G.

Figs. 2544/2545
A pair of seated spaniels with lockets and collars and puppies on their backs and between their feet on a shaped oval base.
HEIGHT: 9.5 inches
PRICE: Pair: C, Singles: F.

Figs. 2546/2547
A pair of seated spaniels on cushioned tasseled bases with puppies begging at their front.
HEIGHT: 6.5 inches
PRICE: Pair: D, Singles: F.

Figs. 2548/2549
A pair of seated spaniels with lockets and collars, on arched gilt lined bases with puppies begging at their front.
HEIGHT: 8.5 inches
PRICE: Pair: D, Singles: F.

Figs. 2550/2551
A pair of seated spaniels with lockets and collars, on cobalt blue gilt lined bases with puppies recumbent at their feet.
HEIGHT: 8 inches
PRICE: Pair: E, Singles: F.

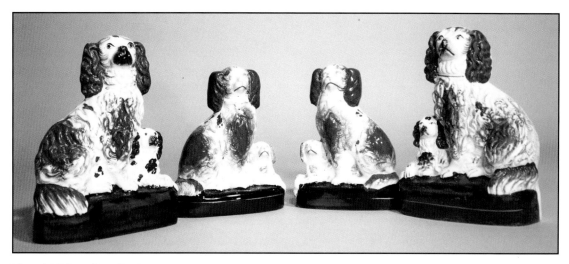

Figs. 2552/2554/2555/2553
Two pairs of spaniels with lockets and collars on cobalt blue gilt lined bases with puppies recumbent at their feet.
At first glance, the larger pair appears identical to Figures 2550/2551, but on closer examination it can be seen that the modelling on this pair is finer and they are larger.
Recently the authors have seen, both in auction houses and at fairs, fakes of the smaller version of these dogs. On the ones seen, the dog is coloured black and the pup red, but this could change. Great care should be taken when purchasing these figures.
HEIGHT: Figures 2552/2553, 8.5 inches
PRICE: Pair: D, Singles: F.
HEIGHT: Figures 2554/2555, 6.5 inches
PRICE: Pair: E, Singles: F.

Figs. 2556/2557
A pair of recumbent spaniels with their pups seated in front.
These are very rare figures.
HEIGHT: 4.75 inches
PRICE: Pair: D, Singles: F.

Figs. 2557A/2557B
A pair of recumbent spaniels on green bases in the form of quill holders.
HEIGHT: 3 inches
PRICE: Pair: F, Singles: G.

Fig. 2557C
A group figure of a seated spaniel and its two puppies, one at its feet, the other on its back, on a shaped gilt lined base.
A very rare and sought after pair of figures. There is a pair for this figure, 2557D has been reserved for it.
HEIGHT: 5.5 inches
PRICE: Pair: D, Singles: F.

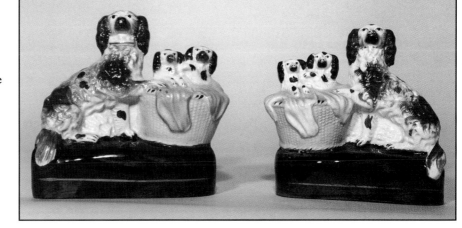

Figs. 2558/2559
A pair of groups of spaniels on cobalt gilt lined bases with their puppies in baskets to the side.
If the dogs are shown in red the puppies are usually decorated in black and vice versa.
HEIGHT: 5.75 inches
PRICE: Pair: C, Singles: E.

Figs. 2559A/2559B
A pair of groups of recumbent spaniels with their pups. These groups are in the forms of trinket boxes. They can also be found with a normal oblong base or a decorated shaped base.
A pair with trinket box bases and singles with normal and shaped bases are illustrated. It is rare to find this pair intact; very often the bases are broken or lost.
HEIGHT: 3.75 inches
PRICE: Pair: E, Singles: F.

Fig. 2560
A group of two spaniels and a puppy on an arched cobalt blue gilt lined base.
This figure was made as a pen holder. The holes for the two pens can be seen on the base.
This group can be found in two sizes, both illustrated , the larger in red and white, the smaller in black and white.
HEIGHT: 5.75 & 4.5 inches
PRICE: D.

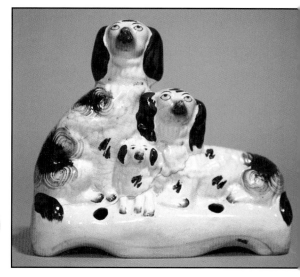

Fig. 2560A
A group of a seated and a recumbent spaniel with a puppy on the back of the seated dog, which has a basket in its mouth, all on an arched cobalt blue base with two holes for quills.
HEIGHT: 5 inches
PRICE: D.

Figs. 2561/2562
A pair of standing spaniels, on yellow lined bases with birds in their mouths.
The potters did not go to the trouble of putting a gilt line on the base, all the colours are enamel and only one firing would have been required, thus producing these figures as cheaply as possible.
HEIGHT: 4.25 inches
PRICE: Pair: G, Singles: H.

Figs. 2562A/2562B
A pair of mirror image group figures with a red and white spaniel seated beside a kennel and a black and white puppy recumbent on top.
HEIGHT: 6.5 inches
PRICE: Pair: E, Singles: F.

Figs. 2563/2564
A pair of seated spaniels, on square tasselled cushion bases.
HEIGHT: 4.5 inches
PRICE: Pair: C, Singles: E.

Figs. 2565/2566
A pair of recumbent spaniels, on oblong arched scrolled bases with puppies feeding.
HEIGHT: 3 inches
PRICE: Pair: F, Singles: G.

Figs. 2567/2568
A very finely modelled pair of spaniels, these figures are porcelaneous.
HEIGHT: 5 inches
PRICE: Pair: D, Singles: F.

Figs. 2569/2570
A pair of spaniels, on yellow lined bases.
This pair was made as cheaply as possible and made to be given away at fairs as prizes.
HEIGHT: 3 inches
PRICE: Pair: G, Singles: H.

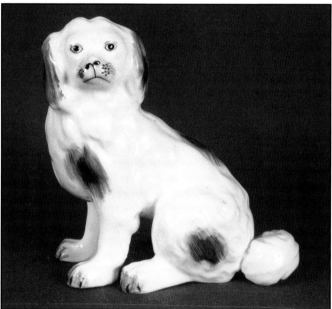

Figs. 2571/2572/2573/2574
A pair of seated spaniels with separate front legs.
These dogs were sold either with or without a base. Their tails can also vary, usually they have a 'pom pom' tail, but a more flattened version can be found.
A single red and white with a base, fig 2571, a single red and white right hand side without a base, both with pom pom tails, and a pair of black and white with flattened tails are illustrated.
HEIGHT: Figs 2571/2572 with base 5 inches, Figs 2573/2574 without base 4 inches
PRICE: Pair: E, Singles: F.

Figs. 2575/2576
A pair of red and white seated spaniels
with a collar locket and separate front
legs, **Figure 2576 not illustrated.**
HEIGHT: 3.5 inches
PRICE: Pair: F, Singles: G.

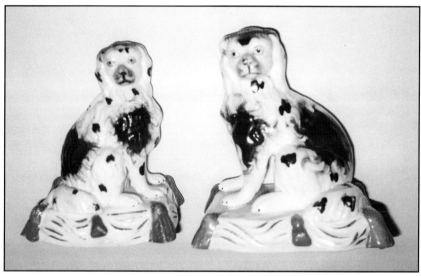

Fig. 2576A/2576B
A pair of spaniels seated on tasseled cushions; in the pair illustrated one dog
is over half an inch larger than the other and has different coloured tassels.
These are therefore a matched pair, and can be found in two sizes.
HEIGHT: 4.5. & 4.75. inches
PRICE: Pair: E, Singles: F.

Figs. 2577/2578
A pair of red and white seated
spaniels with a collar locket,
Figure 2577 not illustrated.
HEIGHT: 4 inches
PRICE: Pair: G, Singles: H.

Figs. 2578A/2578B
A pair of standing black and white spaniels.
These figures are unusual in so far as both dogs have their tongues hanging out. Why dogs should have been portrayed thus is a mystery.
HEIGHT: 5 inches
PRICE: Pair: F, Singles: G.

Figs. 2579/2580
A pair of seated spaniels with separate front legs, **Figure 2580 not illustrated**.
HEIGHT: 4 inches
PRICE: Pair: G, Singles: H.

Figs. 2580A/2580B
A pair of seated spaniels with collars and lockets.
Whilst the two figures illustrated are a pair, they are a matched pair. The same dog was made with different bases, the blue base being the more attractive of the two.
HEIGHT: 6 inches
PRICE: Pair: E, Singles: F.

Figs. 2581/2582
A pair of seated spaniels, on
cobalt blue arched bases.
HEIGHT: 4 inches
PRICE: Pair: G, Singles: H.

Figs. 2582A/2582B
A pair of figures of spaniels
seated on cushions; below
the spaniel a cat is recum-
bent.
A very rare pair of figures.
HEIGHT: 6 inches
PRICE: Pair: C, Singles: E.

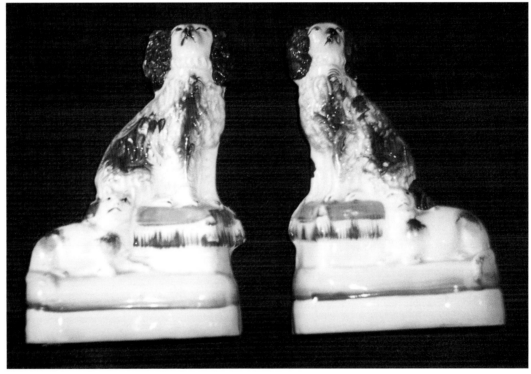

Figs. 2583/2584
A pair of black and white
seated spaniels with separate
front legs, on cobalt blue gilt
lined bases, each with one
forepaw on a dead bird.
HEIGHT: 4.75 inches
PRICE: Pair: E, Singles: G.

Fig. 2585
A doubled headed figure of a spaniel with a recumbent spaniel on the lid, **this was produced for use as a tobacco jar. Reproductions of this figure are being made, but the dog on the lid has been removed and a knop substituted.**
HEIGHT: 6 inches
PRICE: F.

Fig. 2586
A group figure of three spaniels seated around a barrel.
This is a very rare figure; the one illustrated is the only one known to the authors.
HEIGHT: 6.5 inches
PRICE: E.

Fig. 2587
A pair of spaniels' heads made for use as window jambs to keep the sash open. They have been said to be furniture rests, but this is unlikely as they are too frail to support heavy furniture.
Two figures illustrated, any two will pair.
HEIGHT: 4.5 inches
PRICE: Pair: E, Singles: G.

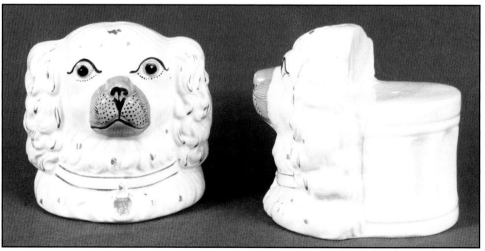

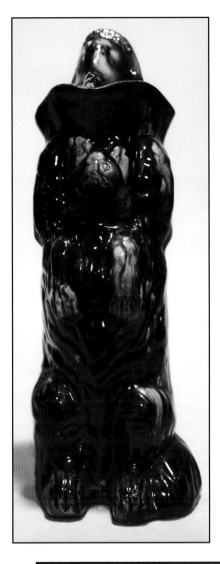

Fig. 2589
A treacle glazed begging spaniel. Made for use as a jug, the "hat" is detachable and is often lost. This figure can be found decorated in red and white, black and white, and white and gilt.
HEIGHT: 11.5 inches
PRICE: F.

Fig. 2590
A figure of a large begging spaniel.
These figures are extremely rare and though two are illustrated they are not a pair, to be a pair the tails would have to curl to either side; both curl to the dog's left. If a pair exists, they are as yet unrecorded.
HEIGHT: 13.5 inches
PRICE: C, Pair (if they exist): A.

Figs. 2591/2592
A pair of figures of seated spaniels, modelled as jugs, these are a true pair as the handles are on opposite sides. **Two pairs illustrated, identical moulds with different decoration.**
HEIGHT: 8 inches
PRICE: Pair: E, Singles: F.

Fig. 2593
A begging spaniel jug with grapes and leaf decoration to the rim, these jugs were made in two sizes, the larger is better modelled; like the begging dog (Figure 2590), there is no pair recorded.
These figures continued to be made well into the 20th century, and illustrated alongside is a 20th century version. It will be noticed that the decoration has no finesse; the figure has been coated with paint rather than decorated.
HEIGHT: 7.25 inches, 10 inches
PRICE: Large: F, Small: G.

Fig. 2594
A group of two seated spaniels, one seated on and chained to a barrel; this was a popular group and a miniature was also made.
This figure can be found in two sizes, both illustrated.
HEIGHT: 8.75 inches, 4 inches
PRICE: 8.75 inches, F; 4 inches, H.

Fig. 2596
A group of two spaniels on either side of a tree stump.
HEIGHT: 5.75 inches
PRICE: G.

Fig. 2597
A group of two spaniels and a Poodle around a clock face.
HEIGHT: 9.5 inches
PRICE: E.

Fig. 2598
A group of a spaniel seated on a cushion, with a Whippet to either side, on an arched base.
HEIGHT: 7 inches
PRICE: E.

Figs. 2598X
A collection of seven single spaniels.
These vary in size from 2.75 inches to 4.75 inches and over the years all have lost their pair. Figures of this
size and quality (or lack of it) are the sort called 'fairings' that would have been given away at fairs as prizes.
PRICE: H.

Fig. 4450
A figure of a King Charles' spaniel recumbent on a cushion with
tassels at all four corners of the cushion.
**The exception that proves the rule! Beautifully modelled and
decorated all around. This extremely rare figure was made by
the Kent pottery in about 1880. The moulds had been reused as
this figure was first made in about 1830. Because the modelling
is so good, it is very difficult to differentiate between early and
late figures and the main guide is that the colouring differs, the
magenta used on the base of the figure illustrated is never seen
on early figures. It is possible that a pair for this figure does
exist – Figure 4449 has been reserved for it. It is however
unrecorded.**
HEIGHT: 7.5 inches
PRICE: B.

Figs. 4451/4452
A pair of seated red and white spaniels with glass
eyes, lockets, and chains. Their tails curl up
behind.
**These dogs are quite rare and unusual in so far
as the red decoration is underglaze, the gilding
is 'bright' gold, the method of applying a red
half hoop to delineate the mouth is quite
distinctive. See figures 4479/4480 for another
pair produced by this factory.**
HEIGHT: 9.75 inches
PRICE: Pair: E, Singles: F.

Figs. 4453/4454
A pair of seated spaniels decorated in red with yellow enamel painted collars and lockets.
These dogs are well decorated and can be found in at least two sizes; they were made in the mid to late 1870s and the potters saved on their production costs by not gilding them at all.
HEIGHT: 5.5 & 8 inches (8 inch pair illustrated.)
PRICE: Pairs: E, Singles: F.

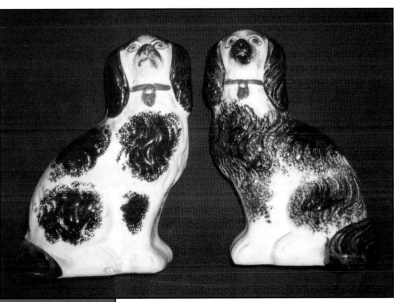

Figs. 4455/4456
A pair of seated spaniels decorated in red with bright gold collars and lockets, and a larger pair decorated in underglaze black.
This model can be found in at least four sizes and differently decorated.
The later production of spaniels showed a decline in the standard of decoration and the feathering that was common on the earlier dogs gradually disappeared and the colour was applied without the finesse previously seen. Compare these figures with Figures 4453/54 and the difference in quality becomes obvious.
HEIGHT: 8.25 & 10 inches
PRICE: Pair: F, Singles: F.

Figs. 4457/4458
A pair of small seated spaniels
with yellow painted collars and
lockets.
**These dogs were made from
simple three part moulds.
Two pairs are illustrated,
identical apart from the
colouring; no gilding has been
applied, thus economising on
the cost of production.**
HEIGHT: 4.5 inches
PRICE: Pair: G, Singles: H.

Figs. 4459/4460
A pair of seated spaniels decorated
in black with copper lustre chains.
**These dogs are well decorated
and can be dated from the
copper lustre chains; they were
made for a considerable period
and earlier versions decorated
with best gold can be found.**
HEIGHT: 8.25 inches
PRICE: Pair: F, Singles: G.

Figs. 4461/4462
A pair of white curly tailed seated
spaniels with painted eyes and
noses.
**There is no trace at all of any
gilding on this pair, either it has
all been lost over the years or it
never had any applied originally.**
HEIGHT: 13 inches
PRICE: Pair: F, Singles: G.

Figs. 4463/4464
A pair of seated spaniels coloured with red decoration, bright gold collars and lockets, and glass eyes with tails curling in front.
Their 'pinched' faces give these dogs an appealing surprised expression and they are well modelled and decorated.
HEIGHT: 13.5 inches
PRICE: Pair: E, Singles: G.

Figs. 4465/4466
A pair of seated spaniels in white and gilt with painted noses.
Bright gold with which these dogs are decorated is much more prone to flaking and often, as in these figures, has almost all disappeared; their noses have been decorated with underglaze black that, in this instance, has run.
HEIGHT: 13 inches
PRICE: Pair: F, Singles: G.

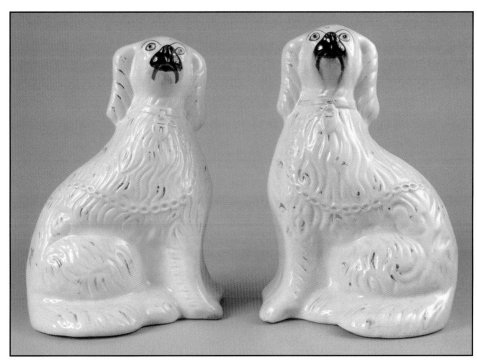

Figs. 4467/4468
A pair of seated spaniels with glass eyes and gilded collars, chains, and lockets.
HEIGHT: 10.5 inches
PRICE: Pair: F, Singles: G.

Figs. 4469/4470
A pair of seated spaniels in white and gilt, these figures have painted eyes and muzzles and a rather truncated curled tail.
They can be found in at least two sizes, both illustrated.
HEIGHT: 12 & 14.5 inches
PRICE: Pair: F, Singles: G.

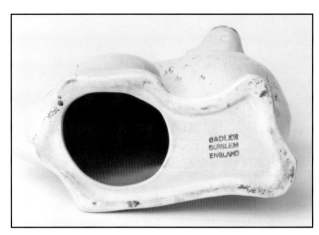

Figs. 4471/4472
A pair of seated spaniels in white and gilt with painted eyes and gilded collars, chains, and lockets, once again decorated with bright gold.

Two pairs are illustrated, they are identical but over the years, probably through overenthusiastic cleaning, most of the gilt decoration on one pair has been lost. This loss will now affect the price, but it is in any event very unusual to find any of these bright gold decorated spaniels with their gilding in original condition. Also illustrated is the base of Figure 4471, which is factory marked 'SADLER BURSLEM ENGLAND.' James Sadler commenced operations in 1899 and a few figures have been found with this mark, which in turn has allowed the attribution of a number of other figures. It can also be seen that this is a slip-moulded figure as the large hole testifies.
HEIGHT: 15.5 inches
PRICE: Pair: F, Singles: G.

Figs. 4473/4474

A pair of seated spaniels in white and gilt with black painted muzzles and eyes, gilded chains, and lockets, and rather truncated tail, and bright gold gilding.

The left hand side figure only is illustrated. This spaniel is similar to Figure 4471 but the modelling and size are slightly different.

When a figure looses its pair it is usually the left hand side figure that is broken. There are far more single right hand side figures surviving than left hand side; this has probably much to do with the fact that most people were right-handed. Being left-handed was actively discouraged, and the left hand side figure would have been picked up with the weaker left hand. This applies to all pairs of figures, not just dogs.

HEIGHT: 12 inches
PRICE: Pair: F, Singles: G.

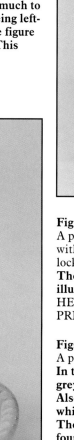

Figs. 4475/4476

A pair of seated spaniels in the white with bright gold gilding on the body, locket, and chain.
The right hand side figure only is illustrated.
HEIGHT: 14 inches
PRICE: Pair: F, Singles: G.

Figs. 4477/4478

A pair of seated spaniels in the white with bright gold gilding.
In this instance, the decorator has added a small amount of grey to delineate the paws.
Also illustrated is a smaller pair of the same model of red and white spaniels with the collars and chains picked out in black. These spaniels were made in at least two sizes and can be found decorated in a variety of colours.
HEIGHT:
11.5 & 13
inches
PRICE: Pair:
F, Singles: G.

Figs. 4479/4480
A pair of seated glass eyed spaniels, decorated with bright gold gilding, the tail curls around to the front rather than erect. **The unusual decoration to these spaniels is the red colour used to delineate the dog's mouths and is very distinctive. These dogs can be found in at least two sizes, 10 inch version illustrated.**
HEIGHT: 10 and 14.5 inches.
PRICE: Pair: F, Singles: G.

Figs. 4481/4482
A pair of seated spaniels, tails curling upwards with painted faces and decorated with bright gold.
Left hand side figure only is illustrated.
HEIGHT: 9.75 inches
PRICE: Pair: F, Singles: G.

Figs. 4483/4484
A pair of seated spaniels with painted faces and very curly tails decorated with bright gold.
These dogs were made in at least three sizes; all are illustrated, although unless illustrated together it is impossible to detect the size difference.
HEIGHT: 9, 9.5, and 12.75 inches
PRICE: Pair: F, Singles: G.

Figs. 4485/4486
A pair of glass eyed seated spaniels with painted faces, lockets, and chains, tails curling around in front.
HEIGHT: 10.5 inches
PRICE: Pair: F, Singles: G.

Figs. 4487/4488
A pair of seated spaniels with lockets, collars, and chains, their tails curled up behind, decorated with bright gold gilding. **These large dogs are well modelled and are similar to the underglaze brown dogs, Figures 4505/4506.**
HEIGHT: 14 inches
PRICE: Pair: F, Singles: G.

Figs. 4491/4492
These late lustre spaniels were made in a number of sizes. Like their earlier counterparts, the small versions do not have chains. Illustrated together are the three most popular sizes, although other sizes can be found.
HEIGHT: 9.75 inches
PRICE: Pair: F, Singles: G.

Figs. 4493/4494
A pair of seated spaniels, with collar, chain, and locket, separate front legs decorated in copper lustre.
Right hand side spaniel illustrated.
These dogs were made for a considerable period; they were first made circa 1850/60 when they were decorated with best gold and were usually either red and white or just in the white with best gold. Manufacture of these figures continued well into the 20th century and when they are found decorated as illustrated in a hard copper lustre they date from 1920-1950.
HEIGHT: 9.75 inches
PRICE: Pair: F, Singles: G.

On occasion the authors have seen catalogued 'A pair of Staffordshire spaniels decorated with green patches'. Spaniels were never decorated with green patches. What has happened is that, due to time and enthusiastic cleaning, the top layer of gold lustre has been cleaned off, leaving the underlying base colour, which is a dull green enamel. Such dogs should be avoided.

Figs. 4495/4496
A pair of seated spaniels with collars and lockets, separate front legs, and decorated in copper lustre patches.
These dogs vary only in size and lack of chain from the previous pair.
HEIGHT: 6 inches
PRICE: Pair: F, Singles: G.

Figs. 4497/4498
A large pair of late lustre spaniels with collars, lockets, and chains are very similar to Figs. 2430/2431, but the base is different and they were made later.
HEIGHT: 12.5 inches
PRICE: Pair: F, Singles: G.

Figs. 4501/4502
A pair of seated glass eyed spaniels.
The underglaze brown decoration is typical of late figures; it is never found on figures made before 1875 and it completely covers the collar, locket, and chain. These are probably later versions of Figures 4485/4486.
Right hand side figure illustrated.
HEIGHT: 11 inches
PRICE: Pair: F, Singles: G.

Figs. 4503/4504
A pair of seated spaniels, the muzzle, collar, locket, and chain highlighted in underglaze black, the whole decorated in under-glaze brown.
No gilding has been used on this pair, as both the colours used are underglaze, no flaking could have occurred.
Right hand side figure illustrated.
HEIGHT: 9 inches
PRICE: Pair: F, Singles: G.

Figs. 4505/4506
A pair of seated spaniels with collars, lockets, and chains decorated in underglaze black, the body in underglaze brown.
These dogs were made in at least two sizes, both illustrated.
HEIGHT: 12 & 13.5 inches
PRICE: Pair: F, Singles: G.

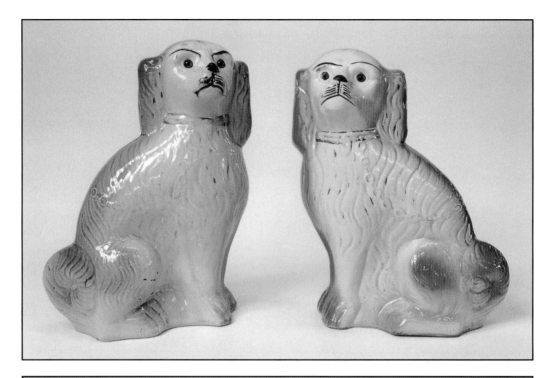

Figs. 4507/4508
A very large pair of seated spaniels with gold collars and lockets.

Two pairs illustrated, one pair decorated in underglaze brown and the other white with bright gold gilding, both pairs have glass eyes.

These are large and impressive dogs that were made by the slip mould method; care was taken with the decoration, each whisker has been separately delineated.

The maker of these dogs is known to be Sadler as a pair has been found with the base of one marked 'SADLER/BURSLEM/ENGLAND.' Sadler did not start in business until 1899, consequently this would have been the earliest that they could have been made.

HEIGHT: 14 inches
PRICE: Pair: F, Singles: G.

Figs. 4509/4510
A pair of figures of seated spaniels with gilded collars, lockets, and chains decorated in underglaze brown with glass eyes.

These dogs are unusual and quite rare; the shape of the ears distinguishes them from other models.

The maker of these dogs is known to be Lancaster and Sons Ltd.; the base of each bears the shield-shaped stamp of this company, a mark that was used by them from circa 1920. This company was formed in 1900 and traded until 1944, when it changed its name to Lancaster & Sandland Ltd., whilst continuing to manufacture from the Dresden Works, Hanley.
HEIGHT: 13 inches
PRICE: Pair: F, Singles: G.

Figs. 4513/4514
A pair of spaniels seated in front of spill vases.

It is rare to find spill vase spaniels; and these figures were first made in the early 1870s, an earlier pair is illustrated (see figures 2526/2527). They were continued in production well into the 20th century.
HEIGHT: 14 inches
PRICE: Pair: E, Singles: F.

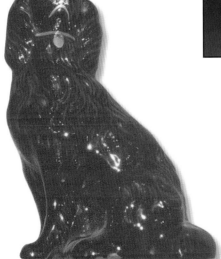

Fig. 4555
A seated spaniel with painted eyes, separate front leg, and a gilt collar and locket.

There is a pair to this figure, a mirror image. Figure 4554 has been reserved for it. Not all 'Jackfield' dogs have a body of red clay, most of those made in Staffordshire have the normal white body, and the potters used existing moulds, so these dogs can be found decorated in red and white, black and white, or just gilded.
HEIGHT: 7.5 inches
PRICE: Pair: F, Singles: G.

Figs. 4556/4557
A pair of seated spaniels with glass eyes, collars, and lockets, in underglaze black.
HEIGHT: 11.5 inches
PRICE: Pair: E, Singles: F.

Figs. 4558/4559
A pair of seated spaniels with glass eyes and collars and chains, tails curled out behind, decorated in underglaze black.
This pair of dogs are the standard size 1 (See figures 2416/2417) with the addition of glass eyes; they were probably made by Samson Smith.
HEIGHT: 12 inches
PRICE: Pair: E, Singles: F.

Figs. 4560/4561
A pair of seated spaniels with glass eyes, lockets, and chains in underglaze black and decorated with bright gold.
These dogs, other than the addition of chains, are the same as Figures 4505/4506; they are also marked 'SADLER' on the base.
HEIGHT: 13.25 inches
PRICE: Pair: E, Singles: F.

Figs. 4562/4563
A pair of seated spaniels, with lockets and chains, decorated in underglaze black and gilt.
This pair is very similar to Figures 4469/4470.
HEIGHT: 15 inches
PRICE: Pair: E, Singles: F.

ii Whippets

Figs. 2600/2601
A pair of standing Whippets, each with three separately moulded legs.
The base decoration on this pair is of a lemon, turquoise, and brown colour that is applied in a particular way. It was also used on many other figures, which would also have been made in the same as yet unknown factory.
HEIGHT: 6 inches
PRICE: Pair: E, Singles: F.

Figs. 2602/2603
A pair of figures of recumbent Whippets, with a dead rabbit at their feet, on shaped and scrolled gilt lined bases.
HEIGHT: 7 inches
PRICE: Pair: E, Singles: F.

Figs. 2604/2605
A pair of spill vase figures of standing
Whippets, with a dead rabbit on each base.
HEIGHT: 8.5 inches
PRICE: Pair: E, Singles: F.

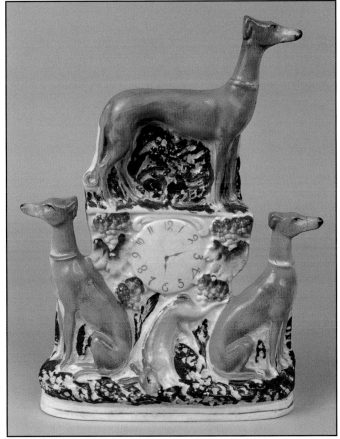

Fig. 2606
A figure of three Whippets, one standing and two seated around a
clock face, with a dead hare below the clock face.
HEIGHT: 11 inches
PRICE: E.

Fig. 2607
A spill vase figure of two Whippets, one standing and the other
crouching, playing with a ball.
**The source or inspiration of this figure was a bronze animalier
figure by Mene, which is virtually identical, other than there is
no spill vase on the bronze. The bronze was exhibited at the
Salon of 1848 and was No. 93 in Mene's catalogue. It was titled
'Groupe de deux leverettes jouant a la boule'. It proved so
popular that both models for this group appear as single
sculptures.
It has been virtually unique to find a source for any of the
Staffordshire dog groups.**
HEIGHT: 7 inches
PRICE: D.

Fig. 2607 SO
A French bronze figure by Mene of
two Whippets playing with a ball.
**This figure is the source to Figure
2607.**

Figs. 2608/2609
A pair of Whippets on
coloured bases with arched
backs, their forepaws resting
on dead hares.
HEIGHT: 6.5 inches
PRICE: Pair: C, Singles: E.

Fig. 2610
A figure of two Whippets standing on their
hind legs on either side of a watch holder
with a hare above.
**Another beautifully constructed group
and very rare.**
HEIGHT: 8 inches
PRICE: D.

Figs. 2611/2612
A pair of standing Greyhounds on titled bases with raised gilt capitals; **whilst these are the only titled pair of dogs figures known, there are two versions of 'Dog Tray' and a portrait of 'Maida' with his owner Sir Walter Scott and a mirror image pair of 'Gelert' with Prince Llewellyn's son. Master McGrath was the most famous Greyhound of the age; he won the Waterloo cup three times, finally in 1871 when he beat Pretender.**
These figures can also be found untitled, as a pair of black or as a pair of brown. They are easily distinguished by the leaf decoration to the supporting column. McGrath is a much rarer figure than Pretender.
HEIGHT: 9.25 inches
PRICE: Pair: A, Pretender: D, McGrath: C.

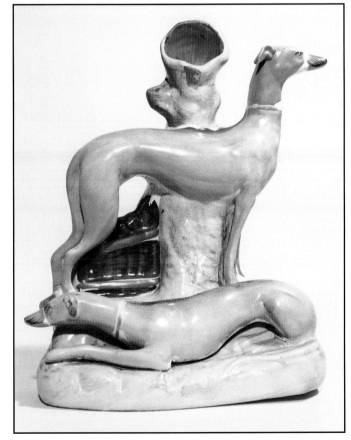

Fig. 2613
A spill vase group of two dogs on a coloured base, one is standing and the other recumbent, to the left of the spill vase there is a small fence. These dogs are usually coloured brown and grey.
It has been suggested that they represent McGrath & Pretender, if so they must date to 1870 at the earliest.
HEIGHT: 11.75 inches
PRICE: E.

Fig. 2614
A rare group of two dogs, one recumbent above the other.
Once again it has been suggested that this group represents McGrath & Pretender. All the examples the authors have seen have been early and it is therefore unlikely that this is so.
HEIGHT: 8 inches
PRICE: E.

Figs. 2615/2616/2617/2618/ 2619/2620
Three pairs of seated Whippets, these dogs are on waisted gilt lined bases and were made in the three sizes shown; all have dead rabbits suspended against the support column.
HEIGHT: Figures 2615/2616, 13.5 inches
PRICE: Pair: C, Singles: E.
HEIGHT: Figures 2617/2618, 9 inches
PRICE: Pair: E, Singles: F.
HEIGHT: Figures 2619/2620, 6 inches
PRICE: Pair: E, Singles: F.

Figs. 2621/2622/2623/2624/2625/2626
Three pairs of standing Whippets, all with rabbits in their mouths; there are two versions of these pairs, the finer version has the dogs standing four square with no support. On the other version, as in Figures 2621/2622 shown, there is a round mound support for the rear legs.
These figures were made for a considerable period, well into the 1900s; the later dogs can be distinguished by two means, firstly the late figures have bright gold on the base line, and secondly late dogs always have grey rabbits in their mouths as opposed to brown in the early ones.
HEIGHT: Figures 2621/2622, 12 inches
PRICE: Pair: E, Singles: F.
HEIGHT: Figures 2623/2624, 9 inches
PRICE: Pair: E, Singles: F.
HEIGHT: Figures 2625/2626, 6 inches
PRICE: Pair: E, Singles: G.

Figs. 2627/2628/2629/2630
Two pairs of standing Whippets with rabbits on the base.
These figures were made in two sizes, and the colouring is always fine with realistic foliage on the bases.
Figure 2629 of the smaller pair is not illustrated.
HEIGHT: Figures 2627/2628, 10 inches
HEIGHT: Figures 2629/2630, 7 inches
PRICE: Pair: E, Singles: F.

Figs. 2631/2632
A pair of recumbent Whippets on cobalt blue bases.
These penholder figures are amongst the most common and popular figures made; many factories produced them and a selection of five pairs follows.
HEIGHT: 5.5 inches
PRICE: Pair: F, Singles: G.

Fig. 2632A/2632B
A pair of figures of recumbent Whippets on shaped blue bases.
We have illustrated a number of these pairs of Whippets. This pair is by far the finest. The modelling is superb, the dogs' ribs are delineated, and the bases are shaped and gilded with scrolls. They are also quill holders.
HEIGHT: 4.75 inches
PRICE: Pairs: E, Singles: G.

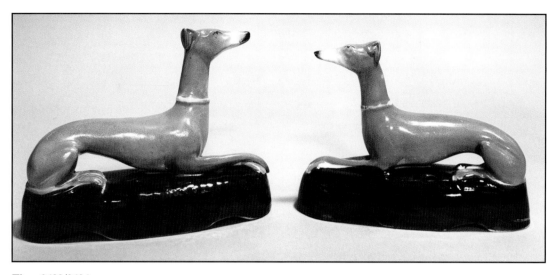

Figs. 2633/2634
A pair of recumbent Whippets on shaped cobalt blue bases.
HEIGHT: 5.5 inches
PRICE: Pair: F, Singles: G.

Figs. 2635/2636
A pair of recumbent Whippets on cobalt blue bases.
HEIGHT: 4.5 inches
PRICE: Pair: F, Singles: G.

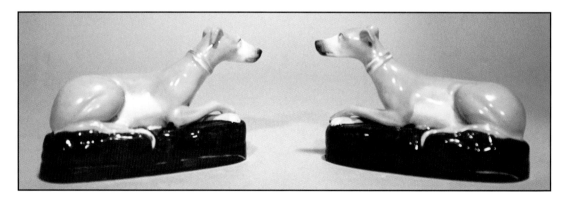

Figs. 2637/2638
A pair of recumbent Whippets on cobalt blue bases.
HEIGHT: 4 inches
PRICE: Pair: F, Singles: G.

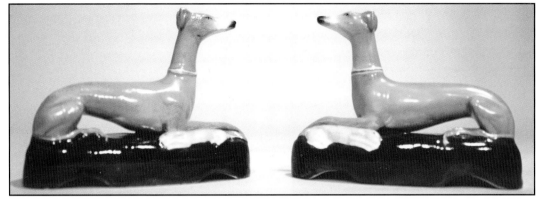

Figs. 2639/2640
A pair of recumbent
Whippets with cobalt blue
bases.
These deviate from the
majority as they have
rabbits on the base.
HEIGHT: 5 inches
PRICE: Pair: F, Singles: G.

Fig. 2640A
A spill vase figure of a recumbent Whippet
before a tree trunk, a dead rabbit at its feet.
**There is a pair to this figure. Figure 2640B
has been reserved for it.**
HEIGHT: 5.75 inches
PRICE: Pair: E, Singles: F.

Fig. 2640C
A spill vase figure of a recumbent
Whippet seated on a cushioned cobalt
blue base.
**There is a pair to this figure. Figure
2640D has been reserved for it.**
HEIGHT: 7 inches
PRICE: Pair: E, Singles: F.

81

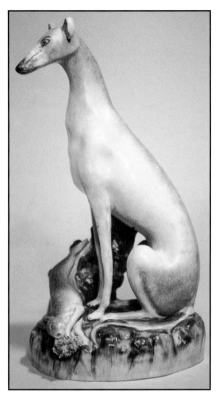

Figs. 2641/2642
A pair of seated Whippets with a hare on the base.
These figures are the product of The Parr Factory.
Figure 2641 not illustrated.
HEIGHT: 12 inches
PRICE: Pair: D, Singles: E.

Figs. 2643/2644
A pair of seated Whippets on cobalt blue bases.
These figures can also be found with the support cut away, with two separate front legs.
These figures can be found in at least two sizes, 7.75 inch version illustrated.
HEIGHT: 7.75 inches, 5.25 inches.
PRICE: Pair: E, Singles: F.

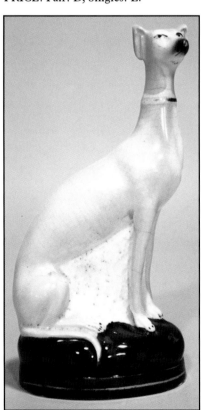

Figs. 2645/2646
A pair of seated Whippets on cobalt blue bases—like Figures 2643/2644, **these can be found with the support cut away.**
The Figure 2646 is not illustrated.
HEIGHT: 8 inches
PRICE: Pair: E, Singles: F.

Figs. 2647/2648
A pair of seated Whippets on coloured shaped bases.
These figures are decorated in the manner of the Parr factory.
HEIGHT: 8.5 inches
PRICE: Pair: D, Singles: F.

Figs. 2649/2650
A pair of seated Whippets on a coloured and lustre base. Figure 2649 is not illustrated.
HEIGHT: 4.25 inches
PRICE: Pair: F, Singles: G.

Figs. 2651/2652
A pair of spill vases of Whippets standing before a fence.
HEIGHT: 7.5 inches
PRICE: Pair: D, Singles: E.

Figs. 2653/2654
A pair of seated Whippets with rabbits at their feet.
HEIGHT: 10 inches
PRICE: Pair: D, Singles: F.

Figs. 2657/2658
A pair of Whippets seated before fences with rabbits in their mouths on cobalt blue bases.
HEIGHT: 9.5 inches
PRICE: Pair: D, Singles: F.

Figs. 2655/2656
A pair of seated Whippets with rabbits at their feet.
These figures are a debased version of Figures 2653/2654 and the potters have not troubled to gild the base. A black line has been drawn around the base instead.
HEIGHT: 9.75 inches
PRICE: Pair: E, Singles: F.

Fig. 2658A
A penholder figure of a Whippet seated by a fence with a rabbit in its mouth.
There is a pair to this figure. Figure 2658B has been reserved for it.
HEIGHT: 5.5 inches
PRICE: Pair: E, Singles: F.

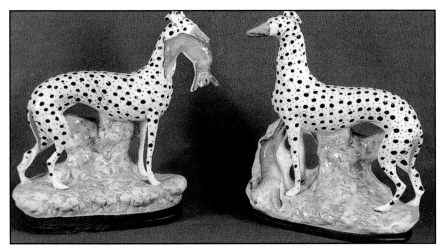

Figs. 2659/2660
A pair of figures of standing Whippets, one with a rabbit in its mouth, the other with it at its feet.

Three pairs are illustrated, two with turquoise and one with a cobalt blue base. Each have been decorated differently, two are very fine, the spotted versions are superb.
HEIGHT: 11.5 inches
PRICE: Pair: C/D, Singles: F.

Figs. 2661/2662
A pair of spill vase
groups of Whippets
chasing rabbits, a
very well constructed
group with the dogs
leaping a fence with a
stream running
below.
**The pair illustrated
is matched, the
figure on the right
being of a later date.**
HEIGHT: 11.5 inches
PRICE: Pair: D,
Singles: F.

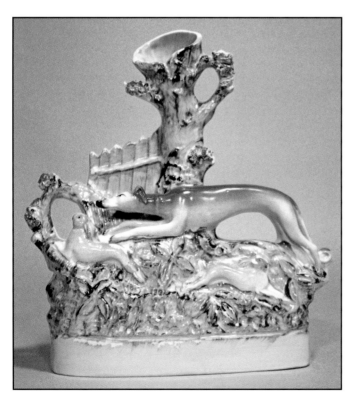

Figs. 2663/2664
A pair of spill vase groups of Whippets chasing rabbits, **Figure
2663 not illustrated.**
HEIGHT: 10 inches
PRICE: Pair: C, Singles: E.

Figs. 2665/2666
A pair of spill vase figures of Whippets chasing rabbits.
Probably the finest version produced.
Figure 2666 not illustrated.
HEIGHT: 12 inches
PRICE: Pair: C, Singles: E.

Figs. 2667/2668
A pair of groups of Whippets, both seated, one with the Whippet looking down at a dead rabbit that lies on the base, the other with its head erect and a spaniel that lays at its feet on the base.
HEIGHT: 6 inches
PRICE: Pair: D, Singles: E.

Fig. 2669/2670
A pair of figures of cobalt blue boxes, their lids having a recumbent Whippet on them, the Whippet forming the lid of the box. Figure 2670 not illustrated.
HEIGHT: 7 inches
PRICE: Pair: E, Singles: F.

Figs. 2671/2672
A pair of recumbent Whippets with rabbits on arched bases.
Three versions are illustrated, identical apart from colouring. These dogs are always beautifully modelled, even the dogs' ribs may be seen.
HEIGHT: 8.5 inches
PRICE: Pair: C, Singles: D.

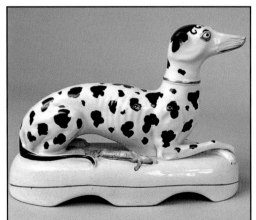

Figs. 2673/2674
A pair of spill vase figures of standing
Whippets with dead rabbits on the base.
**Although decorated with black spots,
these dogs are clearly Whippets.**
HEIGHT: 6.5 inches
PRICE: Pair: D, Singles: E.

Figs. 2675/2676
A pair of spill vase figures of standing
Whippets, one with a dead rabbit in its mouth,
the other with the rabbit laying on the base.
Both spills are adorned with flowers and
leaves, all on a cobalt blue base.
HEIGHT: 9 inches
PRICE: Pair: D, Singles: E.

Figs. 4570/4571
A pair of seated
Whippets with
hares on the base.
**Left hand side
figure illustrated.**
HEIGHT: 7
inches
PRICE: Pair: E,
Singles: F.

Fig. 2677
A spill vase figure of a Whippet standing with
a rabbit in its mouth. The base to the top of
the spill is decorated with a trailing climber.
**There is a pair to this figure; number 2677A
has been reserved for it.**
HEIGHT: 6 inches
PRICE: Pair: E, Singles: F.

iii. Alsatian

Figs. 4515/4516
A pair of recumbent Alsatians decorated in underglaze brown.
The omission of the base is a later innovation and is reminiscent of mid-twentieth century figures made by Sylvac and other twentieth century potters.
HEIGHT: 4 inches
PRICE: Pair: F, Singles: G.

iv. Bull Mastiff

Figs. 2678/2679
A pair of spill vase figures of Bull Mastiffs recumbent.
HEIGHT: 6.75 inches
PRICE: Pair: D, Singles: F.

v. Dalmatians

Figs. 2680/2681
A pair of figures of seated Dalmatians with separate front legs on cobalt blue gilt lined bases.
HEIGHT: 7 inches
PRICE: Pair: E, Singles: F.

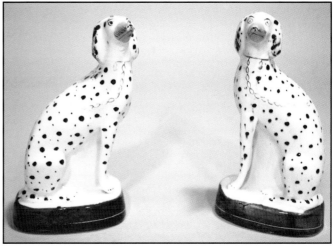

Figs. 2684/2685
A pair of figures of seated Dalmatians on cobalt blue bases, these are not as fine as the Figures 2680/2681/2682/2683 as the legs have been left supported.
HEIGHT: 7.5 inches
PRICE: Pair: E, Singles: F.

Figs. 2682/2683
A pair of figures of seated Dalmatians with separate front legs on cobalt blue gilt lined bases.
HEIGHT: 5 inches
PRICE: Pair: E, Singles: F.

Figs. 2686/2687
A pair of figures of seated Dalmatians, on cobalt blue lined bases.
HEIGHT: 7.5 inches
PRICE: Pair: F, Singles: G.

Figs. 2688/2689
A pair of seated Dalmatians on cobalt blue gilt lined bases.
These have holes on the base and were designed as penholders. They can be found in two sizes, 5 inch version illustrated.
HEIGHT: 5 & 6 inches
PRICE: Pair: F, Singles: G.

Figs. 2690/2691
A pair of seated Dalmatians on cobalt blue bases, also penholders, similar to Figures 2688/2689 but larger. Figure 2691 not illustrated.
HEIGHT: 6 inches
PRICE: Pair: E, Singles: F.

Figs. 4550/4551
A pair of figures of standing Dalmatians on oval bases.
These figures were made in the Kent factory; a single left hand side figure is illustrated, as well as a pair. The single was made earlier and a comparison of the decoration on the base shows how the decoration deteriorated; the single was made in about 1880 and the colours have been applied with a 'combed' effect. By 1950, when this pair was produced combing had been abandoned and the colour applied as a coating with little skill or finesse.
HEIGHT: 6.25 inches
PRICE: Pair: E, Singles: F.

vi. Game Dogs

Figs. 2692/2693
A pair of seated game dogs on oval gilt lined bases.
The figure illustrated on the left is badly damaged and has not been repaired. The price indicated would be for an undamaged pair.
HEIGHT: 5 inches
PRICE: Pair: E, Singles: F.

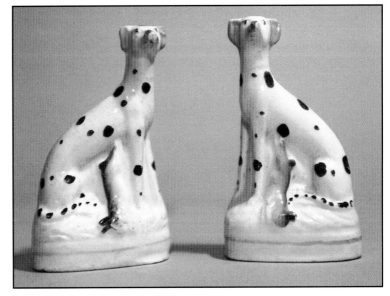

Figs. 2694/2695
A pair of game dogs on yellow lined bases with rabbits between their feet.
HEIGHT: 5.5 inches
PRICE: Pair: F, Singles: G.

Figs. 2696/2697
A pair of groups of game dogs on arched cobalt blue bases, one recumbent, the other seated above him.
HEIGHT: 6.5 inches
The authors have subsequently examined thoroughly a pair of these figures and are of the opinion that they are twentieth century reproductions; similar pairs can be found without the dogs seated behind, by the same hand. Both pairs were first seen in the 1970s. Some examples have impressed numbers on the bottom that are not seen on nineteenth century Staffordshire. It is possible that they are being made on the Continent; they have to date fooled many into believing that they are genuine nineteenth century Staffordshire.

Figs. 2698/2699
A pair of figures of pointers standing on coloured shaped bases.
HEIGHT: 4.75 inches
PRICE: Pair: E, Singles: F.

Figs. 2700/2701
A pair of figures of pointers with tree trunks behind.
HEIGHT: 4.75 inches
PRICE: Pair: E, Singles: F.

Figs. 2700A/2701A
A pair of spill vase figures of pointers.
**These figures appear later than Figures 2700/2701, of which they are a variant; the models
have been adjusted, as the tails would have been particularly vulnerable to damage.**
HEIGHT: 6.5 inches
PRICE: Pair: D, Singles: E.

Figs. 2702/2703
A pair of figures of pointers with their tails curled standing four square on turquoise coloured bases.
HEIGHT: 6 inches
PRICE: Pair: D, Singles: F.

Figs. 2704/2705
A pair of spill vase figures of pointers with a dead bird on the base.
HEIGHT: 6 inches
PRICE: Pair: E, Singles: F.

Figs. 2704A/2705A
A pair of spill vase figures of standing pointers with four separate legs.
These dogs are identical to Figs. 2704/2705, except for the dead birds and the clumps of clay that have been omitted.
HEIGHT: 6 inches
PRICE: Pair: E, Singles: F.

Figs. 2706/2707
A pair of spill vase figures of standing game dogs before trees, Figure 2707 has a dead bird on the base.
These are a matched pair as the decoration to both the dog and the background are different.
HEIGHT: 9 inches
PRICE: Pair: D, Singles: E.

Figs. 2707A/2707B
A pair of spill vase figures of standing game dogs. Figure 2707A is not illustrated.
An extremely rare pair of dogs.
HEIGHT: 7.5 inches
PRICE: Pair: D, Singles: E.

Figs. 2708/2709
A pair of spill vase figures of standing game dogs on cobalt blue gilt lined base, standing before trees with birds in their mouths.
HEIGHT: 10 inches
PRICE: Pair: C, Singles: E.

Figs. 2709A/2709B
A pair of spill vase figures of standing game
dogs with a bird in their mouths, the spill
being decorated with a spray of flowers.
Figure 2709A not illustrated.
HEIGHT: 9.5 inches
PRICE: Pair: E, Singles: F.

Figs. 2710/2711
A pair of game dogs,
probably Newfound-
lands, with four sepa-
rately moulded legs
standing above a tree
stump.
This pair can also be
found with children
standing in front of them,
see Figures 602/603.
HEIGHT: 6 inches
PRICE: Pair: D, Singles:
E.

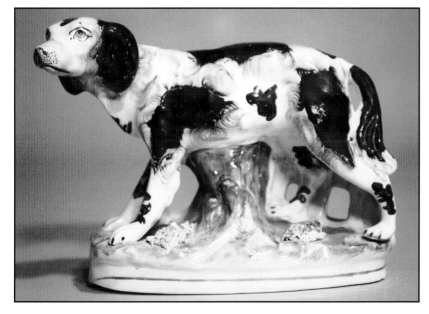

Figs. 2712/2713
A pair of game dogs standing,
probably Springer Spaniels,
Figure 2712 not illustrated.
HEIGHT: 6.75 inches
PRICE: Pair: B, Singles: D.

Figs. 2714/2715
A pair of game dogs on gilt scrolled arched bases, probably Irish Setters, seated with a dead bird on the base.
HEIGHT: 9.25 inches
PRICE: Pair: C, Singles: E.

Figs. 2716/2717
A pair of game dogs seated on gilt scrolled bases, probably Irish Setters. This pair is similar to Figures 2714/2715, but the bases are different and there are no birds.
HEIGHT: 11 inches
PRICE: Pair: A, Singles: D.

Figs. 2718/2719
A pair of group figures of an Irish Setter and a King Charles Spaniel on coloured arched bases, one seated, the other recumbent.
These figures can be found in two sizes.
HEIGHT: 10 inches, 8.25 inches
PRICE: Pair: D, Singles: E.

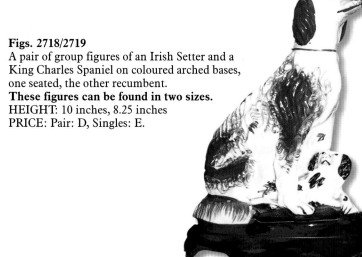

Figs. 2720/2721
A pair of figures of game dogs seated with a dead bird on the base.
HEIGHT: 5 inches
PRICE: Pair: D, Singles: E.

Fig. 2722
A figure of a dog standing four square above a reclining deer. Although it would appear that there should be a pair to this figure, one has never been recorded. Every figure so far seen has been a left hand side figure.
HEIGHT: 9.25 inches
PRICE: E.

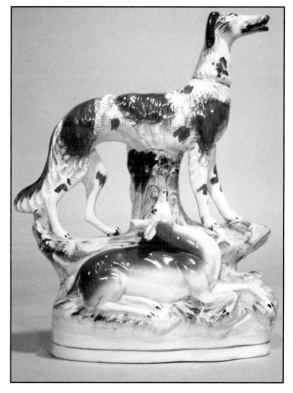

Figs. 2722B/2722C
A pair of spill vase groups of dogs seated to the side of the spill, on which are large decorated leaves. Below two sheep are recumbent.
An extremely rare and very attractive pair of figures.
HEIGHT: 9.5 inches
PRICE: Pair: C, Singles: E.

Figs. 2724/2725
A pair of figures of seated dogs.
These figures are not a true pair, for if original, they would be of the same colour.
HEIGHT: 5 inches
PRICE: Pair: E, Singles: F.

Fig. 2724A
A seated figure of a dog with a pup.
There is a pair to this figure. Figure 2725A has been reserved for it. This figure is very similar to Figure 2724, with the addition of a puppy.
HEIGHT: 5.5 inches
PRICE: Pair: E, Singles: F.

Figs. 2726/2727
A pair of figures of seated dogs with baskets of fruit on waisted bases.
This figure can be found in two sizes. The 6.5 inch version is illustrated.
HEIGHT: 6.5 and 5 inches
PRICE: Pair: E, Singles: F.

Figs 2726A/2727A
A pair of figures of seated dogs with cats to their sides.
These figures are similar to Figures 2726/2727, other than the basket of fruit has been removed and a cat added. Cats in Victorian Staffordshire are quite rare and priced accordingly.
HEIGHT: 6.5 inches
PRICE: Pair: D, Singles: E.

Figs. 2728/2729
A pair of figures of standing dogs
with its paw on a dead bird,
Figure 2729 not illustrated.
HEIGHT: 3.75 inches
PRICE: Pair: F, Singles: G.

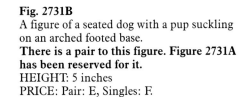

Figs. 2730/2731
A pair of pen and candleholder figures
of a standing dog, on arched gilt lined
bases, **Figure 2730 not illustrated.**
HEIGHT: 4.5 inches
PRICE: Pair: F, Singles: G.

Fig. 2731B
A figure of a seated dog with a pup suckling
on an arched footed base.
**There is a pair to this figure. Figure 2731A
has been reserved for it.**
HEIGHT: 5 inches
PRICE: Pair: E, Singles: F.

Figs. 2731C/2731D
A pair of figures of recumbent dogs on gilded, scrolled cobalt blue bases.
HEIGHT: 6 inches
PRICE: Pair: D, Singles: E.

Figs. 2732/2733
A pair of figures of dogs with their mouth open and tongue protruding standing on concave gilt lined bases, **Figure 2733 not illustrated.**
HEIGHT: 4.5 inches
PRICE: Pair: F, Singles: G.

Fig. 2733B
A figure of a seated dog with a chain lead and a bowl below on a gilt lined cobalt blue base.
There is a pair to this figure. Figure 2733A has been reserved for it.
HEIGHT: 5.5 inches
PRICE: Pair: E, Singles: F.

Figs. 2733C/2733D
A pair of figures of seated hounds, one upright with his head turned to the left with a collar and chain that is attached to the base, the pair is crouching with its chain lead also attached to the base. All are on inverted cobalt blue and gilded bases.
This pair is virtually identical to Figs 2733A/2733B, other than there is no bowl on the base.
HEIGHT: 4.5 inches
PRICE: Pair: C, Singles: E.

Figs. 2734/2735
A pair of dogs recumbent on gilt scrolled bases, **Figure 2735 not illustrated.**
HEIGHT: 3.75 inches
PRICE: Pair: F, Singles: G.

Fig. 2735B
A figure of a dog recumbent on an oblong, gilt lined base, with its head in its forepaws and a large chain around its neck that overlaps the base.
There is a pair to this figure. Number 2735A has been reserved for it.
HEIGHT: 4 inches
PRICE: Pair: D, Singles: F.

Figs. 2736/2737
A very fine pair of dogs, on shaped gilt scrolled bases; whilst differently coloured they are certainly an original pair, and from their design made quite early in the 1830s.
HEIGHT: 3.5 inches
PRICE: Pair: C, Singles: D.

Fig. 2738
A very rare spill vase group of a Bloodhound and Pointer chasing a rabbit down a burrow. Made by the Parr pottery in the early 1850s. Later Kent versions can be found.
HEIGHT: 7.5 inches
PRICE: D.

Figs. 2739/2740
A pair of crouching dogs with birds in their mouths. **This pair is, in the author's opinion, amongst the finest pairs produced. They are extremely rare, beautifully and accurately modelled, full of movement and life. They epitomize the best of Staffordshire.**
HEIGHT: 8 inches
PRICE: Pair: A, Singles: C.

Fig. 2741
A group figure of two game dogs seated above a dead deer.
HEIGHT: 7.5 inches
PRICE: F.

Fig. 2741A
A figure of a dog recumbent on a grassy mound with leaves and flowers. The figure is in the form of a tureen, the base of which is moulded in basket weave.

A very unusual figure, these tureens can be found with hens and other birds on the lid. There is a very rare series with wild animals, but the authors have not seen one with a dog on the lid before. It may well be unique.
HEIGHT: 9 inches
PRICE: E.

Fig. 4552
A seated figure of a Skye terrier decorated all over in an under-glaze brown. In 1858, a man named John Gray died and was buried at old Greyfriars Churchyard. Being a poor man, no headstone was laid; one of the mourners at his funeral was his dog 'Bobby.' The grave was closed in as usual, but the next morning 'Bobby' was found lying on the newly made mound. The grave-yard prohibited dogs and 'Bobby' was driven out, but next morning he was there again, and for a second time he was driven out. The third morning was cold and wet and the curator, James Brown, took pity on him and gave him food and water. From that night on, he never spent a night away from his master's grave. Often in bad weather attempts were made to keep him indoors, but by dismal howls he succeeded in making it known that he wanted to sleep on his master's grave. At almost any time during the day, he could be found in or about the churchyard and stayed there for *fourteen* years until his death in 1872.
TITLE: GREYFRIARS BOBBY
HEIGHT: 7 inches
PRICE: F.

vii. Pekinese

Figs. 4521/4522
A pair of figures of seated Pekinese dogs, decorated both in the white and with under-glaze brown decoration. **Illustrated is a pair in the white and a single decorated with underglaze brown. This figure was made by the slip mould method, and a vent hole the size of an old English penny is usually found in the base.**
HEIGHT: 7 inches
PRICE: Pair F, Singles G.

Figs. 4524/4525
A figure of a Pekinese dog seated on a cushion that has tassels at its corners.
This figure is one of a pair, Figure 4525 not illustrated. Once again, glass eyes, bright gold, and the red/brown decoration date this pair to the 1880s and later.
HEIGHT: 14 inches
PRICE: Pair: C, Singles: D.

Figs. 4526/4527
A pair of figures of standing Pekinese dogs with bows around their necks.
**Two pairs illustrated, they are more often found with the red/brown decoration,
and it is very unusual to find them in black and white with a coloured base.**
HEIGHT: 7.5 inches
PRICE: Pair: F, Singles: G.

viii. Poodles

Fig. 2742
A figure of three Poodles standing and seated around a clock face on an arched base.
HEIGHT: 7.5 inches
PRICE: E.

Figs. 2743/2744
A spill vase pair of standing Poodles chained to a kennel, each with one of their front legs
raised, resting on the kennel.
These figures are a matched pair, as a true pair would have similar coloured bases.
HEIGHT: 8.5 inches
PRICE: Pairs: D, Singles: F.

Figs. 2744A/2744B
A pair of spill vase figures of Poodles by fences, on gilt lined cobalt blue bases. These are mirror images of each other, with one Poodle recumbent and the other seated looking upwards to a tree, where a cat is seated with a dead bird.
HEIGHT: 8 inches
PRICE: Pair: D, Singles: E.

Figs. 2745/2746
Two pairs of seated Poodles with their pups, these groups are usually on cobalt blue bases. **These figures can be found in at least three sizes. The 'fur' on the dogs illustrated was made by passing the clay through a sieve and applying it to the dog's body. These figures may also be found without such decoration, the fur being moulded into the figure. There are illustrated a pair of 7 inch figures without applied fur, and a single 8 inch with fur applied.**
HEIGHT: 8 inches, 7 inches, 6 inches
PRICE: Pair: E, Singles: F.

Figs. 2747/2748
A pair of seated Poodles,
Figure 2748 not illustrated.
HEIGHT: 10.25 inches
PRICE: Pair: F, Singles: G.

Figs. 2749/2750
A pair of seated Poodles with two separate front legs. **The 'woolley' effect was achieved by passing clay through a sieve and applying prior to firing.**
HEIGHT: 8.5 inches
PRICE: Pair: E, Singles: G.

Figs. 2751/2752
A pair of figures of Poodles with their forepaws on barrels in which are pups on cobalt blue gilt lined bases.
HEIGHT: 5.5 inches
PRICE: Pair: E, Singles: G.

Figs. 2753/2754
A pair of Poodles seated on shaped cobalt blue gilt lined bases.
HEIGHT: 4.5 inches
PRICE: Pair: G, Singles: H.

Figs. 2755/2756
A pair of Poodles with flower baskets in their mouths, a very small pair, almost miniature.
HEIGHT: 3.75 inches
PRICE: Pair: G, Singles: H.

Figs. 2759/2760
A pair of figures of a Poodle and puppy recumbent on a cobalt blue cushion base, **Figure 2760 not illustrated.**
HEIGHT: 3.5 inches
PRICE: Pair: F, Singles: G.

Figs. 2757/2758
A pair of Poodles seated on cobalt blue bases, **Figure 2757 not illustrated.**
HEIGHT: 5.5 inches
PRICE: Pair: G, Singles: H.

Figs. 2761/2762
A pair of figures of Poodles recumbent with their front paws on a dead bird on a cobalt blue gilt lined bases, **Figure 2761 not illustrated.**
HEIGHT: 3.5 inches
PRICE: Pair: G, Singles: H.

Fig. 2762B
A group figure of a seated Poodle with its paw raised and placed on a covered table on which a cat sits with a bowl in front of it. **There is a pair to this figure. 2762A has been reserved for it.**
HEIGHT: 4 inches
PRICE: Pair: E, Singles: F.

Figs. 2763/2764
A pair of figures of Poodles recumbent.
HEIGHT: 2 inches
PRICE: Pair: F, Singles: G.

Figs. 2765/2766
A pair of figures of Poodles standing on their hind legs with their front paws on a tree stump, **Figure 2766 not illustrated.**
HEIGHT: 4 inches
PRICE: Pair: F, Singles: G.

Figs. 2767/2768
A pair of seated Poodles on shaped gilt scrolled bases.
HEIGHT: 5 inches
PRICE: Pair: F, Singles: G.

Fig. 2768A
A group figure of a seated Poodle and three pups on a gilt scrolled base.
This figure is very similar to Fig 2767 with the addition of the puppies. There is no doubt a pair to it. Fig. 2768B has been reserved for it.
HEIGHT: 5.5 inches
PRICE: F.

Figs. 2769/2770
A pair of seated Poodles on shaped gilt scrolled bases, these are the same dogs as the preceding Figures 2767/2768 but the base has been changed to a penholder.
HEIGHT: 5 inches
PRICE: Pair: F, Singles: G.

Figs. 2770A/2770B
A pair of figures of standing Poodles, each with four separate legs, facing left and right, with their tails curled, each on a shaped base, and both decorated with shredded clay to simulate fur. **These figures are porcelaneous and were made in the 1830s.**
HEIGHT: 5 inches
PRICE: Pair: E, Singles: F.

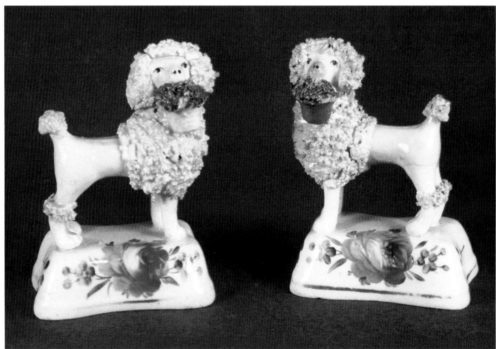

Figs. 2771/2772
A pair of standing Poodles with baskets of flowers in their mouths, the bases are beautifully decorated, painted with a rose.
HEIGHT: 3.5 inches
PRICE: Pair: F, Singles: G.

Figs. 2772A/2772B
A pair of standing figures of Poodles with bags in their mouths and shells on the base
HEIGHT: 3.5 inches
PRICE: Pair: D, Singles: F.

116

Figs. 2773/2773A
A pair of standing Poodles on cobalt blue bases.
These figures are a variant of Figures 2771/2772.
HEIGHT: 3.5 inches
PRICE: Pair: E, Singles: F.

Figs. 2774/2774A
A pair of figures of Poodles and their pups on cobalt blue bases.
HEIGHT: 2.75 inches
PRICE: Pair: E, Singles: F.

Figs. 2774B/2774C
A pair of figures of Poodles standing on cobalt blue bases with
dead birds in their mouths.
HEIGHT: 6 inches
PRICE: Pair: E, Singles: F.

Figs. 2774D/2774E
A pair of quill holder figures of Poodles standing on cobalt blue bases with flower baskets in their mouths.
These figures are very similar to figures 2774B/2774C other than the addition of holes to the bases and the replacement of dead birds with flower baskets.
HEIGHT: 6 inches
PRICE: Pair: E, Singles: F.

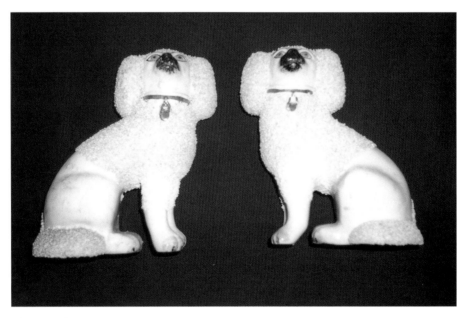

Figs. 4548/4549
A pair of figures of seated Poodles, with painted eyes and muzzles, gilded collars and lockets, and two separate front legs.
The decoration on these dogs gives the impression of fur. It was made by passing clay through a sieve and then applying it prior to firing. They were made for a period both before and after 1875. These figures may be found decorated with either best or bright gold. They can also be found in at least three sizes and four variations (See Figures 2747 - 2750).
HEIGHT: 6.5 inches
PRICE: Pair: F, Singles: G.

ix. Pugs & Bulldogs

Figs. 2775/2776
A pair of standing pugs on coloured gilt lined bases.
With identifiable breeds of dogs such as pugs, some owners of such breeds, whilst not necessarily collectors of Staffordshire, avidly seek these figures; consequently, increased prices are paid for such dogs.
HEIGHT: 9 inches
PRICE: Pair: D, Singles: E.

Figs. 2776A/2776B
A pair of seated Pugs.
These figures were made by the 'slip mould' method and are hollow based. They are circa 1900 and were made in a one part mould. They could not be simplified any further, and by this time other colours were available to be 'underglaze' so that the colours applied could not flake.
The bottom of one of the figures is illustrated to show this method.
HEIGHT: 6 inches
PRICE: Pair: G, Singles: H.

Figs. 2777/2778
A pair of recumbent Pugs.
Whilst late circa 1870-1880, these
are attractive and well modelled.
HEIGHT: 5.5 inches
PRICE: Pair: G, Singles: F.

Figs. 2779/2780
A pair of seated Pugs, these figures have
no bases and are late; they are however
very well modelled and much sought
after.
HEIGHT: 11 inches
PRICE: Pair: D, Singles: F.

Figs. 2780A/2780B
A pair of seated Pugs.
**These figures have no bases and are late.
They appear to be a smaller version of
Figures 2779/2780, but are not so well
modelled.**
HEIGHT: 10 inches
PRICE: Pair: E, Singles: F.

Figs. 2780C/2780D
A pair of seated Pugs, facing left and right, both have two separate front legs and their collars are bows.
These figures were made by the slip mould method in circa 1890.
HEIGHT: 8 inches
PRICE: Pair: F, Singles: G.

Figs. 2781/2782
A pair of seated Pugs facing left and right, both have two separate front legs and no base.
These dogs always have bright gold on their collars and made by the slip mould method, circa 1890.
HEIGHT: 10 inches
PRICE: Pair: E, Singles: F.

Figs. 2783/2784
A pair of standing Pugs, also late figures, the first of these were made in the early 1870s.
HEIGHT: 6.5 inches
PRICE: Pair: F, Singles: G.

Figs. 2785/2786
A pair of standing Pugs, these dogs also have bright gold collars,
Figure 2785 not illustrated.
HEIGHT: 4.5 inches
PRICE: Pair: F, Singles: G.

Figs. 2787/2788
A pair of Pugs seated on cushion bases, **Figure 2788 not illustrated.**
HEIGHT: 3.5 inches
PRICE: Pair: F, Singles: G.

Fig. 4542
A seated figure of a Bulldog with two separate front legs and glass eyes, decorated in an underglaze light beige and dark brown.
A very appealing figure and very well modeled, two figures are illustrated but they are identical, and any two will make a pair. These are very rare figures.
HEIGHT: 7.5 inches
PRICE: F.

Figs. 4544/4545
A pair of seated pugs, each with a separately moulded front leg. **These figures were made by the slip mould method.**
HEIGHT: 4.5 inches
PRICE: Pair F, Singles H.

Figs. 4546/4547
A pair of seated Pugs on oblong shaped bases with curled tails and glass eyes.
This dog is one of a pair, left hand side figure not illustrated; Figure 4546 has been reserved for it.
HEIGHT: 11 inches
PRICE: Pair: F, Singles: G.

Figs. 4564/4565
A pair of figures of seated Pugs with a separate front leg and collars decorated in an underglaze beige and brown. These figures were made by the slop mould method and there is a large hole in the base. **These dogs are very similar to Figs. 4544/4545, the main difference being a larger collar.**
HEIGHT: 5 Inches
PRICE: Pair: F, Singles: H.

123

x. Unidentified Breeds

Figs. 2789/2790
A superb pair of standing dogs, probably terriers, supported with reeded columns on arched cobalt blue bases.
These dogs are superbly modelled and decorated and extremely rare. They are similar to 'Billy the Rat Catcher' (See Figure 2810).
HEIGHT: 8 inches
PRICE: Pair: A, Singles: D.

Figs. 2791/2792
A very rare pair of pipe smoking dogs seated on gilt scrolled bases.
The inspiration for pipe smoking dogs was an oil painting by Landseer titled 'A Quiet Pipe' which became a Pears print.
HEIGHT: 10 inches
PRICE: Pair: A, Singles: D.

Figs. 2792A/2792B
A pair of figures of seated dogs on under glaze blue
bases, both smoking pipes with two separate front legs
and upright curly tail.
Figure 2792B not illustrated.
These are probably small versions of Figs 2791/2792.
HEIGHT: 8 inches
PRICE: Pair: C, Singles: D.

Figs. 2793/2794
A pair of spill vase figures of dogs recumbent
on waisted gilt lined bases, probably Collies.
HEIGHT: 10.25 inches
PRICE: Pair: B, Singles: C.

Fig. 2794A
A spill vase figure of a dog standing four square on
a coloured rococo style base.
**There is a pair to this figure. Figure 2794B has
been reserved for it. An extremely rare figure.**
HEIGHT: 11.5 inches
PRICE: Pair: B, Singles: C.

Figs. 2795/2796
A pair of figures of seated dogs, probably Collies.
HEIGHT: 7 inches
PRICE: Pair: E, Singles: F.

Figs. 2797/2798
A pair of figures of seated dogs, **Figure 2798 not illustrated.**
HEIGHT: 5.5 inches
PRICE: Pair: E, Singles: F.

Fig. 2798A
A figure of a seated dog on a cobalt blue base.
This is a larger variant of Figure 2797. There is a pair to this figure. Figure 2798B has been reserved for it.
HEIGHT: 11 inches
PRICE: Pair: C, Singles: D.

Figs. 2799/2800
A pair of standing figures of Terriers, these figures are unusual in so far as they have no bases at all.
They are late, possibly as late as 1880.
HEIGHT: 6 inches
PRICE: Pair: F, Singles: G.

Fig. 2801
A spill vase group of a dog chained to a kennel, on titled base with raised black capitals, attempting to reach a monkey that is seated on a barrel.
This figure is an adaptation of a pre-Victorian porcelain figure that is smaller and not titled.
Only two examples of this figure have been recorded and the one illustrated is damaged, very unusual, and extremely rare.
TITLE: DON'T YOU WISH YOU MAY GET IT
HEIGHT: 7 inches
PRICE: D.

Fig. 2801A
A penholder figure of a dog and a cat sitting by a table.
This figure may represent a circus act.
HEIGHT: 5 inches
PRICE: E.

Fig. 2802
A figure of a dressed dog, it has been
suggested that this represents 'Punch's'
dog, 'Toby'. It is in the form of a jug.
HEIGHT: 10.5 inches
PRICE: F.

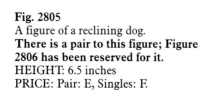

Figs. 2803/2804
A group of a dog in a basket with its
puppies.
**There is a pair to this group but it is of a
cat with her kittens. Figure 2804 has been
reserved for it.**
HEIGHT: 4.75 inches
PRICE: E.

Fig. 2805
A figure of a reclining dog.
**There is a pair to this figure; Figure
2806 has been reserved for it.**
HEIGHT: 6.5 inches
PRICE: Pair: E, Singles: F.

Figs. 2807/2808
A selection of miniature dogs, none more than 3.5 inches high. Many examples were produced. There is often a larger version. On their own they are innocuous, but a whole collection has a great deal of charm when seen together.
HEIGHT: 1.5 to 3.5 inches
PRICE: Pair: G, Singles: H.

Fig. 2810
A figure of a standing dog with a collar around its neck. On the base lay two dead rats. **There is a pair that is a mirror image. Figure 2809 has been reserved for it. This figure is reputed to be of 'Billy the Rat Catcher', who gained his reputation by killing 100 rats in under six minutes. Setting dogs against a number of rats in a pit was a popular poor man's sport in the 1800s. There is another version of this pair, the main difference being that they are 7.5 inches high and there is only one dead rat on the base, and the dog has his front paw on it. Figures 2811/2812 have been reserved for them.**
HEIGHT: 6 inches
PRICE: Pair: D, Singles: E.

Fig. 2813
A spill vase figure of a recumbent dog on a coloured base. **There is a pair to this figure. Figure 2813A has been reserved for it. A number of similar figures were made by this potter, with different animals below the spill.**
HEIGHT: 6 inches
PRICE: Pair: E, Singles: F.

Fig. 2814
A figure of a monkey with his right hand raised to his head, seated on the back of a dog.
HEIGHT: 4 inches
PRICE: E.

Figs. 2815/2815A
A pair of figures of 'Wolf dogs' seated on rocky bases. These figures are porcelaneous and very well modelled.
HEIGHT: 9.5 inches
PRICE: Pair: D, Singles: E.

Fig. 2816
A figure of a seated dog, probably a Collie, with a separate front leg on a raised gilt lined base.
HEIGHT: 6 inches
PRICE: Pair: E, Singles: F.

Fig. 4523
A figure of a begging dog.
This figure incorporates the new innovations of the late 1870s, glass eyes, bright gold, and a red/brown decoration.
This figure is particularly well modelled and very rare. Although two figures are illustrated, they are in fact identical figures with different decoration, any two will make a pair; another example of the economy of the potters, for to make a pair the tail would have to curl to the other side, making another mould necessary.
HEIGHT: 14 inches
PRICE: D.

Figs. 4528/4529
A pair of dogs standing four square without a base, collars around their necks.
This pair is similar to the other models produced, but the modelling of the ears differs. The figures illustrated are very early from the mould and care has been taken in their decoration, the red half hoop decorated mouth is similar to Figures 4479/4480.
HEIGHT: 10 inches
PRICE: Pair: E, Singles: F.

Figs. 4530/4531
A pair of standing dogs with collars and lockets.
These dogs are quite well modelled, separate moulds being used for the legs and tail. This is a departure from the usual three-mould figure; a late Victorian innovation was the dispensing of the base, allowing the figures to stand on their own feet.
HEIGHT: 9 inches
PRICE: Pair: E, Singles: F.

Figs. 4532/4533
A pair of standing dogs, probably St. Bernard's.
These dogs are very well modelled and attractively decorated.
HEIGHT: 9 inches
PRICE: Pair: E, Singles: F.

Figs. 4534/4535
A pair of standing dogs, they are similar to Figures 4530/4531 other than the size and shape of the head. These also have glass eyes; the potter was no doubt attempting to portray another breed. **Illustrated are both a pair of black and white dogs and a single right hand side brown and white dog. These can also be found undecorated in white and gilt.**
HEIGHT: 11 inches
PRICE: Pair: E, Singles: F.

Figs. 4536/4537
A pair of dogs standing on four legs without a base.
These figures are very similar to the preceding pair, probably being just a smaller version, they do not however have collars and lockets, and the eyes are painted.
HEIGHT: 5.5 inches
PRICE: Pair: F, Singles: G.

Figs. 4538/4539
A pair of seated dogs, probably Collies, chains around their neck and shoulders, inset glass eyes decorated partly in underglaze brown.
One glass eye is missing from the right hand side dog; when this occurs they are often replaced with modern plastic teddy bear eyes.
HEIGHT: 13 inches
PRICE: Pair: E, Singles: F.

Figs. 4566/4567
A pair of group figures, the left hand side figure is of a dog seated outside a kennel, on the roof of which a cat is seated, a large fence is behind; the right hand side figure is of a dog chained to his kennel with his front paws on the fence on top of which the cat is seated.
An amusing pair and unusual in so far as very few new pairs of animal groups were made in the 1880s.
HEIGHT: 6.5 inches
PRICE: Pair: E, Singles: F.

Chapter Two
Children with Dogs

Children with animals took sentimentality to the extreme and the potters were happy to produce what the public wanted. At one time or another nearly every figure of a child with an animal has been attributed as being of one of the Royal Children. These attributions were usually made for commercial reasons, as up until recently portrait figures fetched more than decorative. However, that situation has now changed, mainly due to the American market, whose collectors are content to collect the figures for their charm and not their personality.

In any event, production of figures of children with dogs continued well after the Royal children had entered adulthood. So, even if the original intention was to portray the Royal children, this was lost in time and figure production continued.

The Royal children are usually recorded in pairs with a variety of animals. Most were made to represent the two first born children, Princess Royal and Prince of Wales, but they were no doubt sold whenever further children arrived.

Figs. 567/568
A pair of figures in the form of quill holders of the Prince of Wales and the Princess Royal seated on cushions with swags and tails, the Prince holding a boat with a spaniel by his side, wearing a jacket, neckerchief, waistcoat, and trousers, the Princess feeding a rabbit with a spaniel to her side, wearing a blouse and skirt.
HEIGHT: 4 inches
PRICE: Pair: E, Singles: F.

Figs. 570/571
A pair of figures of the Princess Royal and the Prince of Wales seated, the Princess holding a spaniel, wearing a plumed hat, blouse, and skirt, the Prince holding a spaniel, wearing a plumed hat, jacket, and trousers.
HEIGHT: 6 inches
PRICE: Pair: E, Singles: F.

Fig. 595
A figure of the Princess Royal seated side saddle holding a spaniel in her right arm, her left to her side, wearing a plumed hat, jacket, scarf, and skirt. Fig. 594 of the Prince of Wales not illustrated.
HEIGHT: 9.5 inches
PRICE: Pair: E, Singles: F.

Figs. 595A/595B
A pair of figures of the Prince of Wales and the Princess Royal on horseback holding dogs, the Prince wearing a hat and long jacket, the Princess wearing a plumed hat, bodice, and skirt.
These figures are very similar to Figures 594/595, and are probably a smaller version.
HEIGHT: 7.5 inches
PRICE: Pair: D, Singles: F.

Figs. 602/603
A pair of figures of the Prince of Wales and the Princess Royal standing in front of St. Bernard's.
The figures illustrated were made by the Kent pottery in about 1880, earlier Parr versions can be found.
HEIGHT: 10 inches
PRICE: Pair: D, Singles: E.

Figs. 609/610
A pair of figures of the
Prince of Wales and the
Princess Royal standing on
circular gilt lined bases,
the Prince with his right
arm to his side with his
hand resting on the top of
a red and white dog, his
left to his waist, wearing a
plumed hat, shirt,
neckerchief, long jacket,
and trousers, with a belt
around his waist, the
Princess with her left arm
to her side resting on the
head of a lamb, her right to
her waist, wearing a
plumed hat, blouse, skirt,
and pantaloons.
The Princess Royal not
illustrated.
HEIGHT: 11.5 inches
PRICE: Pair: D, Singles:
E.

Fig. 604A
A group figure of the Prince of Wales and the Princess Royal in a
pony cart on a titled base. The Princess is standing with one arm
around a spaniel, which is seated by her side.
HEIGHT: 8.25 inches
PRICE: D.

Figs. 2221/2222
A large pair of figures of
red and white spaniels
on underglazed blue gilt
lined bases, towering
over the children
standing beside them.
**Probably the finest
pair of dog and
children's groups to
have been produced.
A smaller 10 inch
version may also be
found, usually sparsely
coloured.**
HEIGHT: 11.35 inches
PRICE: Pair: A,
Singles: C.

Figs. 2223/2224
A pair of figures of red and white spaniels, on moulded grape and vine leaf bases with children on the dog's back and birds perched on the children's shoulders.
HEIGHT: 10 inches
PRICE: Pair: C, Singles: E.

Fig. 2225
A figure of a spaniel, on moulded grape and vine leaf base with a child on its back and a bird on his shoulder, the child holding a flag above the dog.
This figure is identical to Figure 2223, other than a flag has been added.
There is a pair to this figure. Figure 2226 has been reserved for it.
HEIGHT: 11 inches
PRICE: Pair: C, Singles: E.

Fig. 2226A
A figure of a girl seated on the back of a dog, holding a flag and a drum, wearing a plumed bonnet, blouse, and dress.
There is a pair to this figure, a mirror image, except the girl is replaced by a boy. Figure 2226B has been reserved for it.
HEIGHT: 9 inches
PRICE: Pair: D, Singles: E

137

Figs. 2226C/2226D
A pair of figures of scantily dressed
children seated on the backs of red
and white spaniels, both hold bows in
one hand and arrows in the other, all
on underglaze blue gilt lined bases.
HEIGHT: 6.25 inches
PRICE: Pair: D, Singles: E.

Figs. 2226E/2226F
A pair of spill vase groups of a boy
and girl seated next to a tree trunk in
which there is a bird's nest. She wears
a brimmed hat coat and long dress.
He wears a hat, coat with collar, and
trousers. A dog lays at their feet.
HEIGHT: 4.5 inches
PRICE: Pair: F, Singles: G.

Figs. 2227/2228
A pair of spill vase figures of a girl and
boy asleep beside a tree in which a
large snake is entwined. At their feet
are two sheep. To her right and his left
a large dog stands with one paw
raised, protecting the children from
the snake.
A very attractive pair of figures, quite
rare and very sought after.
HEIGHT: 11.25 inches
PRICE: Pair C. Singles D.

Figs. 2230/2229
A pair of figures of a boy and girl seated above clock faces, which are encircled by flowers and foliage, to their sides two dogs sit, by her Spaniels, by him Poodles, both with flags above them. They both hold a feeding bowl in both hands. She wears a blouse and long skirt. He sits cross-legged with a drum at his feet and wears a shirt and skirt.
A matched pair, he is illustrated in the white, she in full colour.
HEIGHT: 11.5 inches
PRICE: Pair: D, Singles: E.

Figs. 2231/2232
A pair of figures of a boy and a girl seated on the back of spaniels.
These figures are a matched pair, to be a true pair the dogs would be the same colour.
HEIGHT: 7 inches
PRICE: Pair: D, Singles: E.

Figs. 2231A/2232A
A pair of miniature figures of a girl
and boy seated on the backs of dogs.
**These figures are miniature
versions of Figures 2231/2232.**
HEIGHT: 4 inches
PRICE: Pair: F, Singles: G.

Figs. 2233/2234
A pair of figures of a boy and girl seated
on the back of spaniels.
**Similar to Figures 2231/2232, other
than the children are wearing hats
and there are stars on the base.**
HEIGHT: 7 inches
PRICE: Pair: D, Singles: E.

Figs. 2235/2236
A pair of figures of
red and white dogs
with baskets in
their mouths and
children on their
backs, also
illustrated in a
single decorated in
black and white.
HEIGHT: 10.5
inches
PRICE: Pair: D,
Singles: E.

Figs. 2237/2238
A pair of figures of a boy and girl, each standing in front of a red and white dog, on arched gilt scrolled bases.
HEIGHT: 8.75 inches
PRICE: Pair: E, Singles: F.

Figs. 2238A/2238B
A pair of figures of a boy and girl standing, the boy with a dog sitting on a pillar to his side, his right arm to his side, his left raised to his chest holding a posy of flowers; the girl in a similar reversed pose, with a cat to her side sitting on the pillar. Both children have their hats lying against the base of a pillar.
HEIGHT: 9 inches
PRICE: Pair: E, Singles: F.

Figs. 2238C/2238D
A pair of figures of a boy and girl standing on either side of a kennel, both wear plumed hats. She has a bodice and dress with an apron in which there are flowers, he wears a shirt and kilt with a scarf over his shoulder and through his arm. On top of the kennel beside her a rabbit sits on its haunches, on the kennel beside him a dog sits on its hind legs and he has one arm around it.
HEIGHT: 7 inches
PRICE: Pair: E, Singles: F.

Figs. 2239/2240
A pair of figures of a boy and girl seated on the backs of spaniels, each has a drum suspended at their waist by a strap over their shoulders. Both figures wear plumed hats, he a shirt with tie, jacket, and trousers, she a bodice and long skirt. Both hold the chain lead of the spaniels that face left and right. By their side is a small table on which is a bowl, each on a shaped gilt lined base.
HEIGHT: 9.5 inches
PRICE: Pair: C, Singles: E.

Figs. 2240A/2240B
A pair of figures of a boy and girl standing, wearing ermine-edged coats, both with a dog to their side which are seated on cushions on a pillar. The boy's right arm is to his side and his left is raised to his chest holding a posy of flowers. The girl is in a reversed pose. A basket of fruit rests at the base of each pillar.
The dress of both figures is very theatrical, and they could very well be fairground entertainers.
HEIGHT: 9 inches
PRICE: Pair: E, Singles: F.

Figs. 2240C/2240D
A pair of figures of a boy and girl standing, the boy with a dog sitting on a pillar to his side, his right hand resting on his hip, his left raised to his chest holding a posy of flowers; the girl is in a similar reversed pose. Both children are dressed in highland attire of hat, tunic, and kilt, with a scarf over their arm and a sash over their shoulder.
HEIGHT: 9 inches
PRICE: Pair: E, Singles: F.

Fig. 2240E
A group figure of a boy seated on the roof of a kennel and a girl kneeling beside it. He wears a plumed hat and long dress. She wears a plumed hat, bodice, and a long skirt. A dog is recumbent, with his head emerging from the kennel.
HEIGHT: 6 inches
PRICE: F.

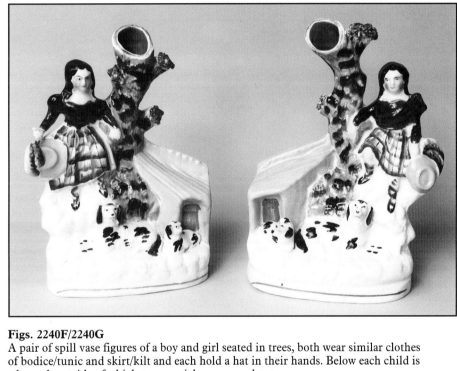

Figs. 2240F/2240G
A pair of spill vase figures of a boy and girl seated in trees, both wear similar clothes of bodice/tunic and skirt/kilt and each hold a hat in their hands. Below each child is a kennel, outside of which two spaniels are recumbent.
HEIGHT: 8 inches
PRICE: Pair: E, Singles: F.

Fig. 2240H
A group figure of a girl standing beside a boy seated on a kennel, he wears a plumed hat, open necked shirt, jacket, and trousers. She wears a hat, bodice jacket, and skirt. A scarf is over her shoulder and through her arm. Below and to the right of the kennel two dogs sit.
HEIGHT: 7.5 inches
PRICE: F.

Figs. 2242/2241
A pair of figures of a boy and a girl seated on top of a kennel with their feet resting on a fence, and a spaniel standing on a barrel, with its paws on the kennel. Each child has an arm around the dog, both wearing plumed hats, she with a blouse, bodice, and aproned skirt; he with a shirt, jacket, kilt with sporran, and a sash over his shoulder and across his chest.
HEIGHT: 8.5 inches
PRICE: Pair: D, Singles: F.

Figs. 2242A/2242B
A pair of spill vase figures of a boy and a girl standing in front of a fence and beside a kennel which has a dog standing on top, both with a hand on the back of the dog and holding hats in the other hand, wearing jackets, skirts, and bloomers.
HEIGHT: 6 inches
PRICE: Pair: D, Singles: F.

Figs. 2242C/2242D
A pair of figures of a boy and girl beside kennels. The boy, with his right leg raised resting on the kennel, is holding a pup in his right hand and a drum in his left, wearing a shirt and kilt. A dog is recumbent to his right in the kennel. His hat is resting on the roof on the kennel. The girl is a reverse image, holding a tambourine in her right hand, a pup in her left, a hat to her left, and wearing a bodice and skirt.
HEIGHT: 6 inches
PRICE: Pair: D, Singles: F.

Figs. 2242E/2242F
A spill vase pair of a girl and a boy seated by kennels, a dog's head emerging from the kennel. The girl is wearing a hat, blouse, and long dress. Her left hand is on the kennel, her right on her lap, and a basket of fruit is to her side. The boy is wearing a hat, frilled collar, and tunic. He has his legs crossed and a basket of fruit to his side.
HEIGHT: 6 inches
PRICE: Pair: E, Singles: F.

Figs. 2242G/2242H
A pair of spill vase groups of a boy and girl seated in a tree above a kennel, both wear plumed hats, tunic/bodice, and kilt/skirt, and have a scarf over their shoulder. A dog sits in their laps. Beside the kennel, a large spaniel sits and a smaller one is recumbent in the kennel.
HEIGHT: 8 inches
PRICE: Pair: D, Singles: E.

Fig. 2242I
A group figure of a girl and boy standing on either side of a kennel, on the top of which is a begging spaniel, with the boy and girl holding a garland of flowers above its head. She is wearing a hat and a long dress. He is wearing a long coat, shirt, breeches, and a scarf across both theirs and the dog's shoulders.
HEIGHT: 7 inches
PRICE: F.

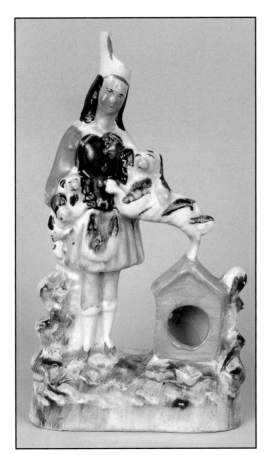

Figs. 2242J/2242K
A pair of figures of a boy and a girl standing beside a kennel, each child holding a puppy under an arm, a dog has its hind legs on the kennel and its front paws on their hips. Both children are dressed in plumed hats, and tunics, he wearing a kilt, she wearing a dress.
The pair illustrated is matched as the bases are differently decorated.
HEIGHT: 8 inches
PRICE: Pair: E, Singles: F.

Figs. 2242L/2242M
A pair of figures of a boy and girl seated on a brick built rabbit hutch. To his left and her right, a spaniel is standing on its hind legs with its paws on their laps. They both wear hats, tunic/blouse, and kilt/skirt. Below and at the entrance to the hutch a rabbit sits, and she holds in her arms another rabbit.
HEIGHT: 8 inches
PRICE: Pair: B, Singles: E.

Figs. 2243/2244
A pair of figures of a boy and girl laying on the back of a red and white dog.
There are two versions of this pair, in one the arm of the child is moulded into the figure; in the other it is a separate mould.
HEIGHT: 8 inches
PRICE: Pair: C, Singles: D.

Fig. 2244A
A figure of a girl seated on the back of a standing dog, the girl with one hand in her lap, the other resting on the head of the dog. She is wearing a plumed hat, blouse, and an aproned skirt.
This figure is a variant of Figure 2244, the main difference being that the girl is seated on the back of the dog, rather than lying. This is the only recorded example of this figure. A pair must have existed once, but at present is unrecorded. Figure 2243A has been reserved for it.
HEIGHT: 9 inches
PRICE: Pair: C, Singles: D.

Fig. 2244C
A group figure of a girl standing dressed in a hat, blouse, and an aproned skirt. Below, another girl is seated on the back of a dog. She is wearing a long dress, her right hand is resting on the dog's head, and her hat is resting by her left hand.
HEIGHT: 10 inches
PRICE: E.

Fig. 2244D
A spill vase figure of a girl seated on rock-work wearing a bodice and long skirt. On her right hand, which is raised to her shoulder, a bird is perched. To her left a dog sits and she has her left hand on its back. The base is rococo and covered in large leaves.
The price given is for the figure in the white, as illustrated. Should a coloured version exist, it would command approximately three times the price.
HEIGHT: 6 inches
PRICE: F.

Fig. 2245
A figure of a boy playing a drum seated on the back of a standing red and white dog.
There is a pair to this figure that is a mirror image, with a girl replacing the boy. Figure 2246 has been reserved for it.
HEIGHT: 7 inches
PRICE: Pair: C, Singles: D.

Figs. 2246A/2246B
A pair of figures of a boy and girl standing in front of a dog. His right arm and her left are raised to the dog's mouth, feeding it. He is wearing a long tunic and a sash around his waist. She wears a long dress with her hat on her back.
HEIGHT: 6.5 inches
PRICE: Pair: D, Singles: E.

Figs. 2246C/2246D
A pair of figures of a boy and girl seated on barrels, a spaniel to their side and another recumbent below. The boy, with both arms around the spaniel, wears a plumed hat, neckerchief, jacket, skirt, and a sash around his waist. The girl, with her right arm around the spaniel and her left resting in her lap, wears a plumed hat, blouse, an aproned skirt, and a sash around her waist.
HEIGHT: 8 inches
PRICE: Pair: D, Singles: F.

Figs. 2246E/2246F
A pair of figures of a boy and girl standing. He wears a plumed hat, frilled shirt, jacket, and knee breeches with a scarf over his shoulder. She wears a plumed hat, bodice, and skirt with an apron and a large scarf is over her shoulder. To one side of them a Poodle sits on a barrel with its forepaws on their waist.
HEIGHT: 8 inches
PRICE: Pair: E, Singles: F.

Fig. 2246G
A figure of a boy seated on a barrel wearing a plumed hat, frilled shirt, tunic, and kilt, with a scarf over his shoulder. His hands are in his lap and there is a drum to his side. To the right of the barrel, a large dog sits on its haunches with its forepaws on the barrel.
There is a pair to this figure. Number 2246H has been reserved for it.
HEIGHT: 9.5 inches
PRICE: Pair: E, Singles: F.

Fig. 2246I
A figure of a boy standing cross-legged wearing a hat, shirt with collar, tunic, and kilt with a scarf through his arm. To his right a barrel sits on steps. On the barrel, a dog sits on its haunches with its forepaws on the boy's waist. The boy has an arm around the dog.
There is a pair to this figure. Number 2246J has been reserved for it.
HEIGHT: 8 inches
PRICE: Pair: E, Singles: F.

Fig. 2247
A spill vase figure of a boy seated with a red
and white spaniel, feeding a bird in the tree.
**There is a pair to this figure that is almost
a mirror image and a girl replaces the boy.**
Figure 2248 has been reserved for it.
HEIGHT: 9 inches
PRICE: Pair: E, Singles: F.

Fig. 2248A
A spill vase figure of a boy seated cross-legged wearing highland
attire, a dog standing to his side, its paw resting on his kilt.
**It is possible that there is a pair to this figure. Figure 2248B has
been reserved for it.**
HEIGHT: 8 inches
PRICE: E.

Fig. 2249
A figure of a seated girl with her arms
around a dog, which is seated to her right.
**There is a pair to this figure; Figure 2250
has been reserved for it.**
HEIGHT: 6 inches
PRICE: Pair: F, Singles: G.

Fig. 2251
A figure of a boy seated astride a recumbent dog.
There is a pair to this figure; Figure 2252 has been reserved for it.
HEIGHT: 4.75 inches
PRICE: Pair: F, Singles: G.

Fig. 2253
A figure of a boy standing cross-legged on a cushion in front of a red and white dog.
There is a pair to this figure that is almost a mirror image, except that a girl replaces the boy. Figure 2254 has been reserved for it.
HEIGHT: 8 inches
PRICE: Pair: D, Singles: E.

Fig. 2255A
A figure of a child standing beside an oversized dog, wearing a blouse, skirt, and knickers, a sash around her waist, holding a large shawl around the dog.
This figure is decorated in the manner of the Parr factory. A rare and desirable figure. Its construction would suggest that there is a pair, although so far it has not been recorded. Figure 2255B has been reserved for it.
HEIGHT: 11 inches
PRICE: D.

Fig. 2256
A figure of a boy standing on rock-work, to his right a girl is seated across the back of a standing spaniel. The boy is wearing a plumed jacket, shirt, and breeches. The girl is wearing a hat, blouse, and an aproned skirt.
HEIGHT: 7 inches
PRICE: E.

Fig. 2256A
A spill vase figure of a boy seated on the back of a dog, with a girl leaning against a tree to his left. She is wearing a blouse, long skirt, and holding a hat in her right hand. He wears a jacket, shirt, waistcoat, and trousers, holding the dog's neck with both hands.
HEIGHT: 10 inches
PRICE: F.

Fig. 2256B
A group figure of a boy and girl seated on rock-work, both wear similar clothing of a brimmed hat, jacket, and kilt/dress. Laying below, with its head raised, is a large dog.
HEIGHT: 6.5 inches
PRICE: E.

Fig. 2257
A group of a boy seated on the back of a red and white dog with a girl seated below holding a black and white spaniel.
It is possible that a pair exists to this figure.
An extremely rare and fine figure.
HEIGHT: 9.25 inches
PRICE: B.

Fig. 2257B
A group figure of a boy and a girl with a dog. The boy is seated on rock-work with the dog resting his front paws on the boy's leg. The girl is standing to his left, wearing a tunic, long dress, and a scarf from which her hat hangs draped over her shoulder and across her arm. He is wearing a plumed hat, tunic, kilt and sporran, and a scarf across his chest.
HEIGHT: 10.75 inches
PRICE: F.

Left:
Fig. 2258
A girl standing cross-legged holding a drum, beside a Poodle seated on its hind legs playing pan pipes.
There is a pair to this figure; Figure 2259 has been reserved for it.
HEIGHT: 8 inches
PRICE: Pair: E, Singles: F.

Right:
Fig. 2259A
A standing figure of a boy dressed in highland attire of plumed hat, blouse with shirt, and kilt with a sash over his shoulder. Perched on his left shoulder is a bird and he holds a bowl in his right hand. To his left, a dog sits begging and behind the dog's head he holds an open book.
This figure and its pair (figure 2259B has been reserved for it) are of circus or theatrical inspiration and no doubt represent a circus act.
HEIGHT: 8 inches
PRICE: Pair: E, Singles: F.

Figs. 2259C/2259D
A pair of arbour figures of a boy and girl seated. Both wear plumed hats, he with a frilled shirt, jacket, knee breeches, and boots, she with a bodice and long skirt. In his right hand he holds a cockerel and his left is on the head of a dog that stands on its hind legs. She holds a chicken in her left hand and her right is on the head of a dog that stands on its hind legs. Below both is a bridge under which a stream runs.
The authors have never seen this pair before. They are very well modelled and constructed. The price given is for them as illustrated in the white. Should a coloured pair exist, the price would be considerably more.
HEIGHT: 10.25 inches
PRICE: Pair: E, Singles: F.

Fig. 2259F
A figure of a girl seated in a chair with her feet on a cushion. She wears a long dress with an apron. A bird is perched on the back of the chair and a spaniel sits on another cushion to her right side.
HEIGHT: 6 inches
PRICE: Pair: E, Singles: F.

Figs. 2260/2261
A pair of figures of a boy and a girl standing cross-legged above clock faces decorated with grapes, each with a begging spaniel on a cushion to their side. The boy is wearing a shirt, jacket, and breeches. The girl is wearing a blouse and skirt, with a sash across her chest.
HEIGHT: 8.25 inches
PRICE: Pairs: D, Singles: F.

Fig. 2261A/2261B
A pair of figures of a girl and boy seated in chairs, both are bareheaded with long hair. She is wearing a blouse and long skirt. Her right hand is in her lap and her left holds a bird aloft. To her right side a spaniel sits on a cushioned stool. The boy is a mirror image.
HEIGHT: 8.5 inches
PRICE: Pair: D, Singles: F.

Fig. 2262
A group of a girl seated in a high-backed chair, dressed in plumed hat, bodice, and long skirt, pouring from a teapot into a cup that is on a table to her side. A dog sits begging on a chair.
There is probably a pair to this figure but is as yet unrecorded. Figure 2262A has been reserved for it. This figure can be found in two sizes both illustrated the larger size being a much finer figure.
HEIGHT: 7 inches, 5.25 inches
PRICE: 7 inch: E, 5.25 inch: F.

Fig. 2262B
A figure of a boy seated wearing a short jacket, kilt with sporran, and a scarf over his right shoulder and across his chest. He holds an open book in his left hand and his right rests on a begging dog that wears a plumed hat and stands on a cushion.
This figure, whilst mainly in the white, is very early from the mould. White and coloured figures were made simultaneously to serve two markets.
HEIGHT: 6 inches
PRICE: E.

Figs. 2263/2264
A pair of spill vase figures of a boy and girl seated with their feet on cushions, holding feeding bowls. To the left of the boy is a begging dog and to the right of the girl a begging cat is also on cushions.
HEIGHT: 7.75 inches
PRICE: Pair: F, Singles: G.

Fig. 2265
An arbour group of a girl seated on a chair, a spaniel beside a table sits on its hind legs begging.
HEIGHT: 7.5 inches
PRICE: G.

Fig. 2265A
A group figure of a boy seated above a bridge under which a swan swims. He wears a plumed hat, frilled shirt, jacket, and breeches. To his right are two large flower pots filled with flowers. To his left, a dog sits begging with a dunces cap on its head. In the boys lap there is an open book.
The significance of the dog with a dunces cap would have to do with the open book on the boys lap, but what exactly it means remains a mystery.
HEIGHT: 8 inches
PRICE: E.

Fig. 2266
A figure of a girl holding a crop seated on the back of a red and white dog.
The style of this figure is early, probably late 1830s or early 1840s.
There is a pair to this figure. Figure 2267 has been reserved for it.
HEIGHT: 6.25 inches
PRICE: E.

157

Figs. 2267A/2267B
A pair of figures of a boy and a girl asleep, the boy lying with a dog standing above and two lambs recumbent below; the girl also lying, with a lamb standing above and two lambs seated below. Above both figures is a large flowering plant.
HEIGHT: 11 inches
PRICE: Pair: E, Singles: F.

Figs. 2267C/2267D
A pair of groups of children seated on the backs of spaniels, both wearing plumed hats, she a blouse and long dress, he a short jacket and trousers. The spaniels have two separate front legs and are all on high rococo bases with two quill holder holes in each.
A very rare pair of figures previously unrecorded.
HEIGHT: 6.25 inches
PRICE: Pair: D, Singles: E.

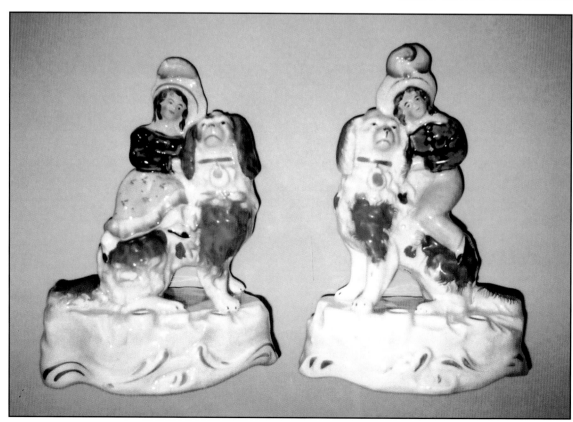

158

Figs. 2268/2269
A pair of figures of a boy and girl seated on the backs of spaniels, each holding a puppy under one arm on cobalt blue arched bases. Both figures are wearing plumed hats. He wears a kilt and she a bodice and a long dress.
A very attractive and sought after pair.
HEIGHT: 6.25 inches
PRICE: Pair: B, Singles: C.

Fig. 2270
A figure of a boy seated on the back of a spaniel.
The figure illustrated is in the white, this figure and its pair, for which Figure 2271 has been reserved, are usually coloured and very desirable; the price given in this instance is for the coloured version.
HEIGHT: 5.5 inches
PRICE: Pair: B, Singles: C.

Fig. 2272
A figure of a girl seated before a begging black and white spaniel, on a titled, gilt lined base with indented black capitals.
An extremely rare figure, decorated in the manner of the Parr factory.
TITLE: BEG SIR
HEIGHT: 5.5 inches
PRICE: C.

Figs. 2273/2274
A porcelaneous pair of figures of a boy
and girl seated on the back of black and
white dogs.
HEIGHT: 6 inches
PRICE: Pair: E, Singles: F.

Figs. 2275/2276
A porcelaneous pair of figures of a boy and
girl seated on the back of black and white
dogs.
HEIGHT: 4.5 inches
PRICE: Pair: E, Singles: F.

Fig. 2276B
A figure of a girl standing cross-legged, a recumbent
Whippet and kennel behind. The girl, with her left hand
raised to her head holding a bird, wears a hat, blouse, a
skirt, and a scarf to her side.
**There is a pair to this figure. Figure 2276A has been
reserved for it.**
HEIGHT: 8.5 inches
PRICE: Pair: E, Singles: F.

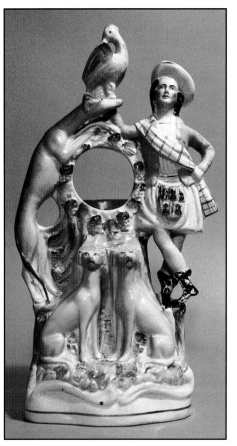

Far left:
Fig. 2277
A group of a boy standing cross-legged on a scrolled, gilt lined base, holding a bird, beside a Whippet that encircles a fob watch holder. Below there are two seated Whippets.
HEIGHT: 13 inches
PRICE: E.

Left:
Fig. 2277A
A figure of a girl standing between two dogs which are seated on cushions, her left hand raised holding a bird, wearing a plumed hat, blouse, a skirt, and a sash across her chest.
It is probable that this figure represents a fairground or similar entertainer. It is possible that there is a pair to this figure. Figure 2277B has been reserved for it.
HEIGHT: 9.5 inches
PRICE: E.

Figs. 2277C/2277D
A pair of spill vase figures of a boy and girl wearing highland attire of plumed hats, cloak, bodice/tunic, and skirt/kilt – he with boots, she with shoes. They both hold a bird aloft and at their feet, to the side, a spaniel sits.
HEIGHT: 9.5 inches
PRICE: Pair: D, Singles: F.

Fig. 2277E
A figure of a boy standing, wearing a frilled shirt with tie, jacket, and kilt, with a scarf over his shoulder. He holds a hat in his right hand and a rabbit aloft in his left. To his right, a dog stands on its hind legs on a cushion.
The boy is standing in a dancing pose and it is probable that this figure depicts a circus act.
HEIGHT: 9 inches
PRICE: E.

Fig. 2278
An arbour group of a boy and girl seated with a dog between them; it has its paws on the girl's lap, she holds a bird aloft and is dressed in bodice and skirt, her hat by her side. The boy wears a shirt, jacket, and trousers, a tied bag is on the base.
HEIGHT: 8 inches
PRICE: G.

Figs. 2278A/2278B
A pair of figures of a boy and girl standing by an arbour in the form of a vine with a Greyhound, with its front paws resting on their waists. He is wearing a hat, waistcoat, shirt, jacket, and trousers. She wears a hat, blouse, skirt, and a scarf over her shoulder and around her back.
HEIGHT: 9.5 inches
PRICE: Pair: E, Singles: F.

Fig. 2278C
An arbour figure of a girl seated between two pillars wearing a blouse and long skirt and holding a bird in her right hand. Against one of the pillars sits a dog.
HEIGHT: 6.25 inches
PRICE: Pair: F, Singles: G.

Fig. 2278E
A figure of a boy standing, wearing a plumed hat, tunic, kilt, leggings, shoes, and socks. A large scarf is draped over both shoulders; he holds a bird on his right shoulder and a spaniel under his left arm.
HEIGHT: 9.75 inches
PRICE: Pair: F, Singles: G.

Figs. 2279/2280
A pair of figures of a girl
and boy seated on the backs
of standing dogs. She wears
a blouse and long skirt, he a
shirt, short jacket, and
trousers. She is seated
sidesaddle, he astride.
HEIGHT: 5.5 inches
PRICE: Pair: E, Singles: F.

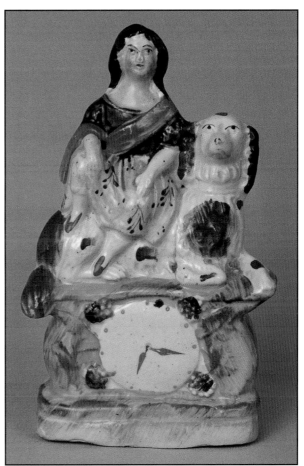

Fig. 2281
A spill vase figure of a seated Scottish boy, playing with a Poodle that
has its paws on his lap, a stream runs below.
There is a pair to this figure. Figure 2282 has been reserved for it.
HEIGHT: 6 inches
PRICE: Pair: F, Singles: F.

Fig. 2282A
A figure of a girl seated on a recumbent dog above a clock
face which is decorated with grapes. She wears a blouse,
skirt, and a sash over her shoulders.
**There is a pair to this figure. Figure 2282B has been
reserved for it.**
HEIGHT: 6 inches
PRICE: Pair: F, Singles: F.

Fig. 2282E
A seated figure of a bareheaded girl wearing a blouse and long skirt with her knickers showing holds a dog on her lap with both hands. **There is a pair to this figure that was made by the 'Alpha' factory. Figure 2282F has been reserved for it.**
HEIGHT: 6.5 inches
PRICE: Pair: F, Singles: G.

Figs. 2282C/2282D
A pair of spill vase figures of a boy and girl standing with one foot raised onto rock-work. Both children are bareheaded with long hair; he wears a long tunic and trousers, she a bodice and long skirt. To their side, on a covered table, stands a dog on its hind legs begging.
HEIGHT: 7.5 inches
PRICE: Pair: E, Singles: F.

Figs. 2283/2284
A pair of figures of girls standing on cushions with baskets in their hands and spaniels seated on cushions to either side of them. **These figures can be found in two sizes, a 6.5 inch coloured and an 8 inch white pair are illustrated.**
HEIGHT: 8 inches, 6.5 inches
PRICE: Pair: E, Singles: F.

Figs. 2284A/2284B
A pair of figures of a girl and boy standing with one foot raised, both wearing a hat, jacket, and skirt/kilt with socks. She holds a garland in her right hand, he in his left. Her left hand and his right rest on a dog, which stands begging on a covered table. This pair can be found in two sizes, a 6.5 inch pair and a single 8 inch figure are illustrated.
HEIGHT: 6.5 inches, 8 inches
PRICE: Pair: E, Singles: F.

Fig. 2285
A figure of a boy standing, wearing a large hat, long coat, and trousers seated with a puppy on his lap.
There is a pair to this figure. Figure 2286 has been reserved for it.
HEIGHT: 6.5 inches
PRICE: Pair: F, Singles: G.

Fig. 2286A
A figure of a boy seated on a large chair, a rifle and dead bird to his side, and a dog recumbent below. He is wearing a plumed hat, jacket, kilt, and a sash across his chest.
There is probably a pair to this figure. It may well be a figure representing a hunter. Figure 2286B has been reserved for it.
HEIGHT: 7 inches
PRICE: E.

Figs. 2287/2288
A pair of figures of a boy and girl standing with a
bird on their shoulders. To her left and his right is a
kennel resting on rock-work on which a spaniel is
recumbent. Both boy and girl are similarly dressed,
wearing a blouse/tunic and kilt/skirt.
HEIGHT: 6.75 inches
PRICE: Pair: F, Singles: G.

Fig. 2287C
A figure of a girl standing, wearing a large brimmed
hat, blouse, skirt, and shoes and socks. A scarf is
draped over her right arm and a Whippet stands on
its hind legs on rock-work to her side with its
forepaws on her left arm.
HEIGHT: 9 inches
PRICE: F.

Figs. 2287E/2287F
A pair of figures of a boy and girl standing, wearing
a hat with feather, she with a jacket and dress. She
holds a garland in her right hand and to her left side
a spaniel stands on its hind legs, around which she
has her left hand. He wears a jacket, open necked
shirt, short trousers tied with a scarf, and knee
boots. A dog stands begging at his left side.
HEIGHT: 9 inches
PRICE: Pair: E, Singles: F.

Figs. 2288A/2288B
A pair of figures of a boy and girl standing to either side of shaped pillars, he wears highland attire of cap, tunic with sash, and sporran. A dog is seated on top of the pillar with its forepaws on the boy's chest and he has his arm around it. She wears a plumed hat, bodice, and long dress. A scarf is over her arm. On the pillar by her side is a pot of flowers on which a bird is perched.
It is possible that these figures portray The Royal Children.
HEIGHT: 6.5 inches
PRICE: Pair: E, Singles: F.

Figs. 2288E/2288F
A pair of figures of a girl and boy, both seated on rock-work. They are dressed similarly with a blouse, skirt/kilt, a bird sits on her right shoulder, and another sits on his left shoulder. A dog is standing on its hind legs with its forepaws in their laps.
HEIGHT: 6.5 inches
PRICE: Pair: F, Singles: G.

Figs. 2288C/2288D
A pair of spill vase figures of a girl and boy, both wearing plumed hats, she with a blouse and skirt tied with a sash and long trousers, he with a tunic with a sash and trousers. They hold a bird in one hand and a basket of flowers in the other; a dog stands on its hind legs at their feet.
HEIGHT: 7.5 inches
PRICE: Pair: F, Singles: G.

Fig. 2289
A figure of a seated, scantily dressed girl on a circular coloured base with her dog by her side.
This figure is decorated in the manner of the Parr factory. There is a pair to this figure. Figure 2290 has been reserved for it.
HEIGHT: 5.5 inches
PRICE: Pair: F, Singles: G.

Figs. 2291/2292
A pair of miniature figures of a boy
and girl seated on the backs of
spaniels.
**Figures of this size were probably
given away at fairs as prizes.**
HEIGHT: 3 inches
PRICE: Pair: G, Singles: H.

Fig. 2292A
A small quill holder figure of a girl seated wearing a long dress
with her left arm around a spaniel. Both are seated on an over
large cushion that forms the holder.
There is a pair to this figure. 2292B has been reserved for it.
It is possible that this pair portray the Royal Children.
HEIGHT: 4 inches
PRICE: Pair: F, Singles: G.

Fig. 2292C
A small quill holder group of a boy and girl seated on a
large cushion. He holds a rose in one hand, she has one
hand in her lap and the other across her chest.
**Whilst there is no dog in this group, it has been
illustrated here as it would appear to be the
centrepiece for Figs. 2292A/2292B.**
HEIGHT: 4 inches
PRICE: G.

Fig. 2292D
A figure of a girl wearing a hat, dress
with an apron, and long skirt, standing
in front of a standing dog.
HEIGHT: 6 inches
PRICE: E.

Figs. 2293/2294
A pair of figures of a boy and girl standing with dogs jumping up at their sides.
HEIGHT: 6.5 inches
PRICE: Pair: G, Singles: H.

Fig. 2294A
A spill vase figure of a girl wearing a plumed hat, blouse, skirt, and a scarf over her shoulder. She is standing beside a dog, holding its lead. A puppy below is climbing on the back of the dog.
There is probably a pair to this figure. Figure 2294B has been reserved for it.
HEIGHT: 8.5 inches
PRICE: G.

Fig. 2295
A figure of a boy standing, wearing a hat, smock, shoes, socks, with a large scarf over his shoulder, holding an object in his right hand and a dog seated by his feet.
There is a pair to this figure. 2295A has been reserved for it.
HEIGHT: 7.5 inches
PRICE: F.

Figs. 2296/2297
A pair of figures of a naked child being protected by a dog with snakes below. In one, the dog is standing with the child sitting beneath it and in the other the child sits on the back of the seated dog.
HEIGHT: 6.5 inches
PRICE: Pair: E, Singles: F.

Figs. 2296/2297 SO
Illustrated is a Baxter print, which shows three statues from The Great Exhibition at Crystal Palace of 1851. The two outside statues depict a dog protecting a child from a snake. These are the sources for Figures a2296/a2297. It is possible that the potter/modeller never saw the original statues and was inspired by the Baxter print.

Fig. 2297A
A figure of a dog protecting a child from a snake, the dog stands with the snake wrapped around its legs. A child wearing only a scarf lays on the ground with one hand on the dog's back. There is a pair to this figure. 2297B has been reserved for it.
HEIGHT: 7.5 inches
PRICE: Pair: E, Singles: F.

Figs. 2299A/2299B
A pair of spill vase figures of a boy and girl seated with small dogs in their laps. Both children wear plumed hats and trousers, he a long coat, she a blouse. He holds a trumpet in his left hand and she a violin in her right. These figures have a quill hole in the base.
HEIGHT: 6.75 inches
PRICE: Pair: E, Singles: F.

Fig. 2298
A spill vase 'Dog, rescue' figure, a dog pulls a drowning child from a stream.
There are a number of variants to this figure, as well as a dog rescuing a child from a snake.
There is a pair to this figure. Figure 2299 has been reserved for it.
HEIGHT: 8 inches
PRICE: Pair: F, Singles: G.

Fig. 2299D
A figure of a child dressed in a robe lying asleep, resting against a recumbent dog all on a rococo base.
There is a pair to this figure. 2299E has been reserved for it.
HEIGHT: 3.5 inches
PRICE: Pair: E, Singles: F.

Fig. 2299F
A figure of a boy, lying asleep on the back of a
seated dog, he wears a short jacket, open necked
shirt, waistcoat, and knee breeches. A large hat and
two objects are by his feet, all on a shaped, scrolled,
and gilded base.
**This is an extremely finely modelled figure and
also bears similarities with a Landseer print.**
HEIGHT: 8 inches
PRICE: E

Fig. 2299D/F. SO
A newly discovered print, titled 'Saved', from a painting by Sir Edwin Landseer; whilst not identical to the figures, it
is near enough to be considered the inspiration. These heroic dog rescue scenes were frequently portrayed in
Victorian genre paintings and it is probable that they inspired the potters to produce similar figures.

Fig. 2300
A group figure of a girl lying asleep, above a large
bird with wings outstretched. A spaniel is to her
side protecting her with its paw raised.
HEIGHT: 8.5 inches
PRICE: F.

Fig. 2300A
A spill vase figure of a child lying asleep, holding a basket, a hat
on the ground by her feet, and a large dog sitting beside her.
HEIGHT: 6 inches
PRICE: E.

Fig. 2301
A spill vase figure of a child seated on an uphol-
stered chair with a dog next to her.
There is a pair to this figure. 2301A has been
reserved for it.
HEIGHT: 8 inches
PRICE: Pair: E, Singles: F.

Fig. 2301B
A figure of a girl standing, wearing a brimmed hat, blouse, and skirt with an apron. Her knickers show below the skirt and in her apron there are bunches of grapes. She holds in her left hand a tambourine that rests on the back of a seated dog.
There is a pair to this figure. 2301C has been reserved for it.
HEIGHT: 6 inches
PRICE: Pair: F, Singles: G.

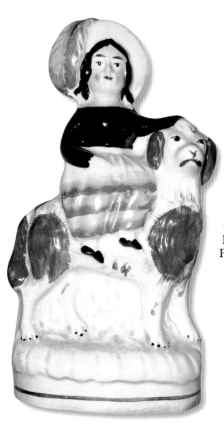

Fig. 2302
A figure of a girl sitting sidesaddle on the back of a standing dog.
There is probably a pair to this figure but it is as yet unrecorded.
HEIGHT: 6.5 inches
PRICE: Pair: F, Singles: G.

Fig. 2303
A figure of a boy standing cross-legged, wearing a plumed hat, jacket, and kilt, on a base in the form of a clock, his right arm resting on his waist, his left raised holding a bird, to his left a dog rests his front paws on his kilt.
There is a pair to this figure. Figure 2304 has been reserved for it.
HEIGHT: 10 inches
PRICE: Pair: E, Singles: F.

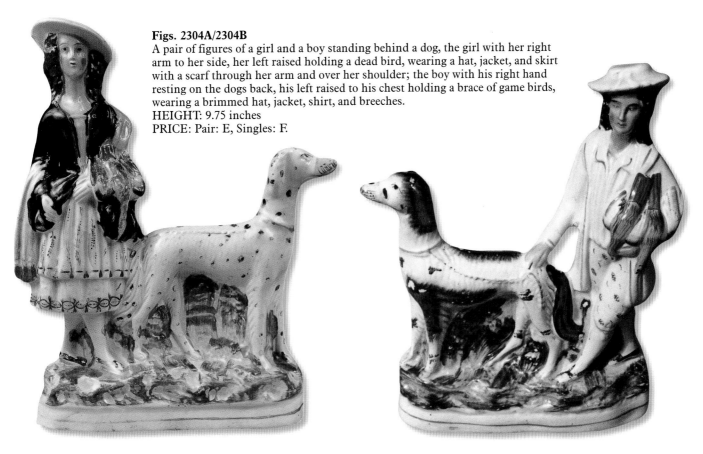

Figs. 2304A/2304B
A pair of figures of a girl and a boy standing behind a dog, the girl with her right arm to her side, her left raised holding a dead bird, wearing a hat, jacket, and skirt with a scarf through her arm and over her shoulder; the boy with his right hand resting on the dogs back, his left raised to his chest holding a brace of game birds, wearing a brimmed hat, jacket, shirt, and breeches.
HEIGHT: 9.75 inches
PRICE: Pair: E, Singles: F.

Figs. 2304C/2304D
A pair of spill vase figures of a boy and girl standing dressed in highland attire, she with a hat, bodice, and skirt with an apron, she holds a large flowered scarf in both hands. He wears a plumed hat, frilled shirt, jacket kilt with sporran, and a scarf across his chest. A water bottle is by his left hand. To his left and her right of a spill sits a large spaniel and on the base of each a sheep is recumbent. **A very well coloured and modelled pair of figures and very desirable.**
HEIGHT: 12 inches
PRICE Pair: D, Singles: E.

Fig. 2305
A group figure of a boy seated on a dog with a girl kneeling below, the boy with his right hand resting on the dog's head, his left holding a basket, wearing a plumed hat, frock coat, and trousers, the girl kneeling with a bowl, wearing a bodice and dress.
An extremely rare figure.
HEIGHT: 7.5 inches
PRICE: C.

Fig. 2305A
A figure of a boy standing beside a standing dog, on which a girl is seated. Both children are dressed in highland attire.
This is a very rare figure, and is similar to Figure 2305. Both may represent the Royal Children, although there is no firm evidence to confirm this.
HEIGHT: 7.25 inches
PRICE: D.

Fig. 2309G/2309H
A pair of figures of a boy and girl standing. He leans on rock-work to his right and wears a plumed hat, frilled shirt, jacket, and knee breeches. To his left on a tree trunk a birdcage stands with a bird perched on top, at his feet a spaniel lays. She is bareheaded and wears a blouse and long skirt, a scarf draped around her. She holds the ends in her left hand, her right rests on two birds that are perched on a pillar beside her. Both rest on a rococo base.
The authors are reasonably certain that the two figures illustrated are a pair, although they have not been seen together. It is, however, possible that there are another two figures that would pair either of these.
The modeller was a consummate artist, certainly one of the best in Staffordshire in the 1850s, the time when these figures were made. All of his figures are comparatively rare and much sought after due to their quality.
HEIGHT: 9 inches
PRICE: Pair: D, Singles: F.

A pair of group figures of a girl seated above a bridge from which a stream flows. She wears a plumed hat, blouse, and a skirt with an apron in which there are flowers. A dog is by her right side with its paws on her lap, a large goat stands on its hind legs with its paws on her shoulder. The pair is almost a mirror image, other than a boy replacing the girl. He wears a plumed hat, shirt, tunic, and kilt with a sporran. A large scarf is over his left shoulder and across his chest.
HEIGHT: 7.75 inches
Price: Pair: E, Singles: F.

Fig. 3345A
A watch-holder figure of a child asleep in a cot, with a cherub above, a dog seated to their side, and a dead wolf below.
This figure is a representation of Gelert and Prince Llewelyn's son. Although no source has been found for this particular figure, there is another similar figure (Figure 3345B has been reserved for it) of a child seated with a dog and a dead wolf below. This figure is a mirror image of an engraving by W. H. Mote after Daniel Maclise (1806-1870) inscribed 'Faithful Gelert'.
The story of Gelert is a mythical tale of a hound given to Prince Llewelyn by King John. The tale is set in the thirteenth century. One day the Prince went hunting and Gelert, his 'faithful hound', was not to be seen. On his return, Prince Llewelyn found his hound covered in blood. The Prince went to find his son, only to find his cot stained in blood. Thinking that his hound had killed his only heir, the Prince plunged his sword into him. The dog's dying yell was answered by the child, who was unharmed. Near to the child was the dead wolf that Gelert had slain. The Prince, on seeing this, was filled with remorse and was said to have never smiled again.
HEIGHT: 11 inches
PRICE: E.

Figs. 3345B/3345C
A pair of figures of a dog seated on a tasseled bench, standing guard over a child who kneels on a cushion beside him, while below a wolf lies dead. Each figure is a mirror image of the other, the only difference being that a girl replaces the boy.
The boy is a representation of Gelert and Prince Llewellyn's son, the girl was made as a balancing figure to make a pair. Both figures are extremely rare.
HEIGHT: 9.5 inches
PRICE: Pair: D, Singles: E.

Chapter Three
Dogs with Their Masters

In this chapter, dogs make their appearance with royalty, shepherds, hunters, musicians … and just about anywhere they can insert themselves.

Fig. 308
A figure of Sir Walter Scott standing with his dog Maida on a titled base with gilt script, his right hand raised to his chest, his left across his chest holding a book, wearing a jacket, neckerchief, and trousers, a sash across his chest and shoulder.
This figure can be found in three sizes, all illustrated.
Very few dogs, other than dogs with the Royal children, appeared in Portrait figures. This is one.
Victorian wool work pictures were also made of Sir Walter Scott, with his dog Maida. In these, the dog is shown as a much larger breed, possible an Elkhound.
TITLE: SIR WALTER SCOTT
HEIGHT: 14.5 inches, 10.75 inches, 9.5 inches
PRICE: E/F.

Fig. 515
A figure of Prince Albert on horseback on a titled base with gilt script, his right arm to his side, his left hand holding the reins, a pair of red and white dogs chasing a stag above a stream below, wearing a top hat, long jacket, and trousers.
A very rare and desirable figure.
The only figure recorded of Prince Albert with dogs, Hunts, usually bear the name of the locality. It has not been recorded that there was ever a 'Royal' stag hunt.
TITLED: ROYAL STAG HUNT
HEIGHT: 10 inches
PRICE: C.

Figs. 627/628
Prince Albert and the Prince of Wales standing on gilt scrolled rococo bases, Alfred beside a tree trunk with his right hand resting on his hip holding a plumed hat, his left across his chest holding a birdcage, wearing a tunic, scarf, neckerchief, breeches, and boots.
The Prince of Wales with his left arm to his side leaning on a pillar, his right hand resting on his hip holding a plumed hat, a black and white spaniel seated on a cushion to his right, wearing a tunic, scarf, breeches, and boots.
A King Charles Spaniel sits on a cushion at the feet of The Prince of Wales. His mother, Queen Victoria, had such a spaniel. Perhaps he borrowed it for the day, as all other figures of him show him with larger dogs.
The finest pair of the Royal Princes produced, and very rare.
HEIGHT: 10.5 inches
PRICE: Pair: B, Singles: C.

Fig. 631
A figure of the Prince of Wales standing on a titled gilt lined base with raised gilt capitals, his right arm to his side leaning on a pillar draped with a cloth, his left hand resting on the head of a red and white spaniel, wearing a jacket, neckerchief, waistcoat, and trousers.
TITLE: PRINCE OF WALES
HEIGHT: 14 inches
PRICE: E.

Fig. 632
A figure of the Prince of Wales standing, his left arm resting against a tree holding a staff, his right hand resting on the head of a red and white spaniel, wearing a plumed hat, tunic, scarf, kilt with sporran, and chequered socks.
HEIGHT: 14.75 inches
PRICE: E.

Fig. 633
A figure of the Prince of Wales standing on a titled gilt lined base with raised gilt capitals, his right arm to his side holding a plumed hat, his left to his side, a red and white dog to his left, wearing a jacket, kilt, sporran, and chequered socks, with a scarf across his chest.
TITLE: PRINCE OF WALES
HEIGHT: 15 inches
PRICE: E.

Fig. 632 SO
An engraving of the Prince of Wales, which appeared in *The Illustrated London News*, the inspiration and identification of Figure 632.

Fig. 635
A figure of the Prince of Wales standing, his right hand to his side resting on the head of a black and white dog, his left to his side holding the barrel of a rifle, wearing a plumed hat, jacket, neckerchief, and chequered trousers.
This figure is decorated in the manner of the Parr factory.
HEIGHT: 11.5 inches
PRICE: E.

Fig. 635A
A figure of the Prince of Wales standing, a dog leaping to his right, wearing highland attire of a bonnet, scarf, jacket, kilt, and stockings.
HEIGHT: 12 inches
PRICE: F.

Fig. 791
Queen Victoria and Victor Emmanuel II standing on a titled base with gilt raised capitals, Victoria with her right arm across her chest, her left to her side holding a handkerchief, wearing a crown, ermine edged cloak, bodice, and long skirt, Napoleon III with his right arm across his chest, his left to his side, a dog between his legs, wearing an ermine edged cloak, tunic, and trousers, a sash across his waist.
A dog has managed to insert himself between the legs of Victor Emmanuel and gazes at Queen Victoria.
TITLE: QUEEN & KING OF SARDINA
HEIGHT: 14 inches
PRICE: F.

Figs. 918/919
A pair of figures of officers mounted on horseback, one hand raised to their caps holding a horn, the other holding a dead fox by its hind legs. A dog lays recumbent on the base.
HEIGHT: 10 inches
PRICE: Pair: D, Singles: E.

'Dog Tray'

A poem published in 1836 by Thomas Campbell entitled *The Harper*, also a song written and composed by the American Stephen Foster.

Old Dog Tray's ever faithful,
Grief cannot drive him away,
He's gentle, he is kind,
I'll never, never find
A better friend than old Dog Tray.

Fig. 1121
A figure of a child with a spaniel seated above on a titled gilt lined base with raised black capitals, the child asleep against a tree with a hoop and stick below, wearing a dress with waisted sash, Dog Tray seated looking on above.
TITLE: DOG TRAY
HEIGHT: 10 inches
PRICE: F.

Fig. 1122
A spill vase figure of a man seated with a black and white spaniel in front of a tree on a titled base with raised gilt capitals, the man cross-legged holding a bag in his left hand, wearing a straw hat, long jacket, neckerchief, waistcoat, and breeches, Dog Tray looking on.
TITLE: DOG TRAY
HEIGHT: 13 inches
PRICE: F.

Fig. 1122A
A spill vase figure of a man seated to the side of a tree, wearing a top hat, shirt with tie, waistcoat, long jacket, and knee breeches. One hand is on his knee and the other holds a handkerchief bundle. To the other side of the tree a spaniel sits on its haunches.
This figure is very similar to Fig 1122 and, although it has never been found titled, it can be considered a smaller version of 'Dog Tray'.
HEIGHT: 8. inches
PRICE: F.

Mother Hubbard

A nursery rhyme by Sarah Catherine Martin (1768-1826), published in 1805. The rhyme tells of Mother Hubbard, whom lived in a cupboard and was too poor to give her dog a bone.

Fig. 1179
A figure of Mother Hubbard standing on an oval base, with a begging black and white spaniel seated on a cushion, a cupboard under her left arm, her right across her chest.
HEIGHT: 9.5 inches
PRICE: F.

Fig. 1378/1379
A pair of figures of a woman and man standing by pillars on rococo style gilt scrolled bases, she is holding a bird to her chest with her left hand, her right hand resting on a pillar, wearing a plumed hat, split bodice, dress, and gloves; he with his right resting on the head of a dog, his left resting on a pillar, wearing a plumed hat, ermine lined cloak, tunic, and pantaloons.
These figures are of exceptional quality, are very rare, and have so far escaped identification, their appearance suggests operatic rather than theatrical. If they are of operatic origin, it would be unlikely to have a dog on stage whilst singing.
HEIGHT: 11 inches
PRICE: Pair: C, Singles: D.

Fig. 1472
A group figure of a man and woman seated, he with his right hand raised to his chest and his left around her. A dog lays on the base, looking up at the couple.
HEIGHT: 8.5 inches
PRICE: F.

Fig. 1473
A group figure of a seated woman and man, with a dog below, which has its front paws resting on the woman's lap. She, with both her arms raised holding a bird, wears a head-scarf, bodice, and long skirt; he, with his left arm around her and his right hand resting on the dog's head, wears a turban, jacket, shirt, and pantaloons.
This figure appears to be another version of Figure 1472.
HEIGHT: 8.5 inches
PRICE: F.

Figs. 1474/1475
A pair of figures of a woman and man, both seated and wearing theatrical costumes of plumed hats and ermine edged coats. She has an apron and pantaloons, he a long tunic. Both hold a bird aloft with their arm resting on a birdcage, which in turn rests on a dog kennel. At their feet, a dog is recumbent. Each is a mirror image of the other.
HEIGHT: 8.5 inches
PRICE: Pair: E, Singles: F.

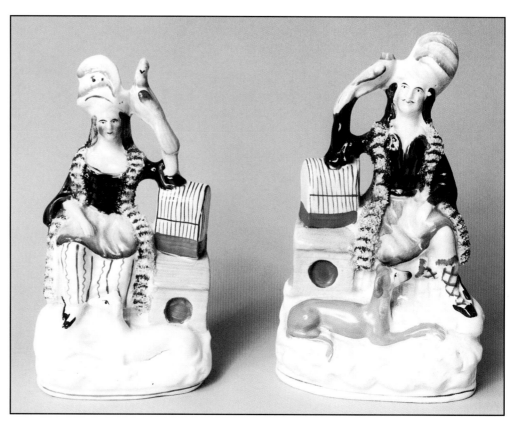

Fig. 1490
A group figure of a man and woman seated cross-legged in a boat, he with his arms to his chest holding a musical pipe, wearing an ermine edged cloak, jacket, shirt, and breeches while she, with one arm in her lap and the other around a dog, wears a bonnet, bodice, and skirt.
HEIGHT: 9.5 inches
PRICE: F.

Fig. 1514A
A group figure of a boy and girl standing on either side of a watch holder, holding a bird aloft. Both children are bareheaded. He wears a jacket and kilt with a scarf over his right shoulder, she wears a jacket, skirt, and a scarf over her arm. A dog sits on the base between them. Both children have their legs crossed in dancing pose.
HEIGHT: 8.5 inches
PRICE: G.

Figs. 1531/1531A
A pair of figures of a man and woman dancing. They both hold garlands of flowers in one hand and a dog in the other. She wears a headdress, bodice, blouse, a skirt with an apron, and a scarf around her waist. He wears a shirt with a large collar over a jacket, knee breeches, and socks with tassels.
HEIGHT: 9.75 inches
PRICE: Pair: E, Singles: F.

Fig. 1554A
A spill vase figure of a man seated wearing a
brimmed hat, scarf, jacket, trousers with frills at
the knees, boots, and an ermine edged cape. He
is playing a stringed instrument with both hands
and to his left his dog is seated. At his feet a goat
is recumbent.
HEIGHT: 12.5 inches
PRICE: E.

Figs. 1588C/1588D
A pair of figures of a man and woman seated on rock-work dressed in highland
attire, he wears a plumed hat, tunic, kilt, and shoes with stockings, a large scarf is
over his shoulders. He is holding and playing bagpipes. A dog sits at attention at
his feet. She also wears a plumed hat, bodice, a long skirt with an apron, and a scarf
over her right arm. Her left hand holds a stringed instrument. A dog sits at
attention at her feet.
HEIGHT: 10.5 inches.
PRICE: Pair: F, Singles: G.

Fig. 1572B
A group figure of a man standing and woman sitting on rock-
work, he wears a plumed hat, frilled shirt with collar, jacket, knee
breeches, and a drum is suspended at his side by a strap over his
shoulder. She wears a bodice and long skirt with an apron, and
holds a stringed instrument in her left hand. Between them, a
spaniel stands on its hind legs and the man has his left arm
around it.
**This group probably represents itinerant musicians with their
performing dog.**
HEIGHT: 8.5 inches
PRICE: F.

Fig. 1591B
A spill vase figure on a scrolled base of a boy standing on rock-work wearing a brimmed hat, smock, and trousers playing a mandolin. A dog lies at his feet.
Two figures, similar apart from decoration, were both made by the 'Green factory' and feature the two base colours that this factory generally used. Figures can also be found with the base left uncoloured.
HEIGHT: 7.25 inches
PRICE: F.

The following three blind musicians all have their faithful dogs in attendance.

Fig. 1592A
A figure of a harpist seated cross-legged with a spaniel standing on its hind legs, its front paws on his chest, and a lamb lying below. The harpist is wearing a plumed hat, jacket, shirt, and breeches.
HEIGHT: 10.5 inches
PRICE: F.

Fig. 1592
A figure of a blind harpist seated cross-legged with a spaniel standing on its hind legs, its front paws on his leg, the harp decorated with two lion's heads, a stick and bundle by his feet, wearing a hat, ermine topped cloak, long jacket, shirt, neckerchief, knee breeches, and boots.
HEIGHT: 14 inches
PRICE: E.

Figs. 1593/1594
A pair of figures of a blind fiddler and woman standing on gilt lined bases, he is holding a stringed instrument in his left hand, a cloth over his arm, is right hand resting on the head of a spaniel, wearing a jacket, waistcoat, neckerchief, and knee breeches, she holding a cane in her right hand a hat in her left, wearing a scarf around her head, cloak, and long dress.
HEIGHT: 11.75 inches
PRICE: Pair: E, Singles: F.

Fig. 1595
A figure of a blind fiddler seated cross-legged on rock-work, with a spaniel to his left, holding a stringed instrument in his right hand, his left resting on his leg, wearing a plumed hat, cloak, jacket, waistcoat, neckerchief, and knee breeches.
HEIGHT: 11.75 inches
PRICE: F.

Fig. 1596
A group figure of a seated highlander with crossed legs wearing a plumed hat, tunic kilt and sporran, socks, and shoes, playing the bagpipes. To his left, a small child stands on a fence and at his feet a dog sits with its paws on his leg.
HEIGHT: 10 inches
PRICE: E.

Fig. 1599
A figure of a man standing cross-legged with a spaniel at his feet, his left hand raised holding a stringed instrument, his right resting on rock-work, holding a hat, wearing a long jacket, shirt, neckerchief, and knee breeches, with a sash around his waist.
HEIGHT: 9.75 inches
PRICE: F.

Figs. 1598B/1598A
A pair of figures of a man and woman standing playing mandolins. He wears a hat, frilled shirt, jacket, and knee breeches with boots; she wears a hat, bodice, and short skirt. To his left and her right there is a cushioned pedestal on which a spaniel reclines.
HEIGHT: 11.5 inches
PRICE: Pair: E, Singles: F.

Figs. 1600/1600A
A pair of figures of a man and woman seated on rock-work, the man with his left arm around a dog, his right to his side holding a stringed instrument. He is wearing a plumed hat, jacket, shirt, neckerchief, knee breeches, and a sash around his waist. The woman, with her right arm around a lamb and a musical instrument to her side, is wearing a head-dress, bodice, and a long skirt.
HEIGHT: 14 inches
PRICE: Pair: F, Singles: G.

Fig. 1606A
A figure of a man seated, holding a stringed instrument, wearing a cloak, jacket, and pantaloons, with a dog lying at his feet.
There is probably a pair to this figure. Figure 1606B has been reserved for it.
HEIGHT: 7.5 inches
PRICE: F.

Fig. 1606C
A spill vase figure of a seated boy wearing an open neck shirt, jacket, and knee breeches with leggings. He is holding and playing pipes with both hands, and his dog sits at his feet begging.
There is a pair to this figure. 1606D has been reserved for it.
HEIGHT: 7 inches
PRICE: Pair: F, Singles: G.

Fig. 1607
A figure of a man standing cross-legged with a spaniel at his feet, on a square base with canted corners, he is leaning on a pillar, holding a wind instrument in his right hand, his left by his side, wearing a plumed hat, jacket, neckerchief, waistcoat, and trousers.
There is a pair to this figure and Figure 1608 has been reserved for it.
HEIGHT: 9.25 inches
PRICE: Pair: E, Singles: F.

Fig. 1623C
A figure of a seated musician playing the bagpipes dressed in hat, overcoat, shirt, and knee breeches. His dog is seated at his feet and the base is of a cut out rococo style.

There are at least three different pairs of these figures in various sizes and all are modelled in the round with a number of subsidiary moulds. It is probable that they are copies of earlier porcelain factory figures.
HEIGHT: 6.25 inches
PRICE: G.

Fig. 1614
A spill vase figure of a man standing cross-legged, with a dog begging at his feet, holding a wind instrument in both hands, a bag and strap across his chest, wearing a plumed hat, jacket, and breeches.
HEIGHT: 9.25 inches
PRICE: F.

Fig. 1623E
A figure of a man standing with his legs crossed wearing a plumed hat, shirt, jacket, pantaloons tied at the waist with a scarf, and short boots. His right arm rests on rock-work and his left holds musical pipes. His dog sits at his left side, all on a rococo base. This figure probably depicts a shepherd.
HEIGHT: 9.5 inches
PRICE: E.

Sighted musicians and street entertainers also had their faithful dogs in attendance.

Fig. 1630
A group figure of a man, woman, and dog, he is sitting with the dog's paws in his lap, wearing a plumed hat, cloak, jacket, and pantaloons, a tambourine at his feet, she is standing with one hand on hip, wearing a plumed hat, bodice, and skirt with a scarf over her arm and holding a violin.
HEIGHT: 13 inches
PRICE: F.

Figs. 1639/1639A
A pair of groups of figures of a man and girl and woman and boy. The man and woman both lean on a grape vine. At their feet, the boy and girl both have spaniels sitting in their laps.
HEIGHT: 11.25 inches
PRICE: Pair: D, Singles: F.

Figs. 1658/1659
A pair of figures of man and woman standing musicians. She holds a harp, which rests on a fence where a bird perches. He holds a stringed instrument in both hands, one foot rests on a fence, and a bird perches on his knee. A dog sits at attention at his feet.
HEIGHT: 8.75 inches
PRICE: Pair: E, Singles, F.

Fig. 1662A
A standing figure of a highlander holding bagpipes dressed in plumed hat, shirt, jacket, kilt with sporran, shoes and socks, with a scarf is over his shoulder. A dog stands at his feet.
HEIGHT: 16.5 inches
PRICE: E.

Figs. 1663/1664
A pair of figures of a man and woman standing cross-legged, the man playing the bagpipes, a dog recumbent below, wearing a plumed hat, tunic, kilt, sporran, and a scarf over his arm. The woman, with both arms raised holding a lamb, wears a plumed bonnet, blouse, long skirt, and a scarf over her arm.
There are a number of pairs of figures where the man has a dog and the woman a sheep. These are usually denoting Shepherds.
HEIGHT: 13.5 inches
PRICE: Pair: E, Singles: F

Fig. 1668A
A spill vase group figure of a standing man with one foot raised on a small brick wall wearing a plumed hat, open necked shirt with a loose tie, jacket, and knee breeches tied with a scarf, holding a stringed instrument aloft in his left hand. A dog sits at his feet and his right hand is placed on the shoulder of a woman who is seated on the wall. She wears a bodice and long skirt with an apron. A stringed instrument rests against her legs.
HEIGHT: 12 inches
PRICE: E.

Fig. 1670D
A figure of a girl standing, playing an organ, a bird perched on the top and a dog recumbent at her feet. She is wearing a blouse and a skirt with a bow on the back.
There is a pair to this figure. Figure 1670E has been reserved for it.
HEIGHT: 11 inches
PRICE: Pair: E, Singles: F

Fig. 1670F
A figure of a boy standing beside a bowl of fruit with a Poodle seated below. The boy holds a squeeze box in both hands and is wearing a brimmed hat, shirt, jacket, cloak, and breeches.
There is a pair to this figure. Figure 1670G has been reserved for it.
HEIGHT: 9 inches
PRICE: Pair: F, Singles: G.

Hunters

Hunting with horses was a pastime for the rich. Other forms of hunting did however proliferate; particularly hunting with guns, although there are figures of hunters with bows, and by far the largest proportion of these figures are clad in highland attire, and none the worse for that. Many of these figures of standing or seated hunters also feature their faithful dog, either seated at their master's feet or jumping up at his side. The animals hunted are also included, and dead deer, stags, otters, boars, and pheasants can be found. The hunting of birds with falcons was also popular. Once again the potters, ever commercial, made figures of mounted and standing falconers. The working class pastime of poaching was not forgotten. Although sometimes carried out by netting, most often successful poaching was achieved with the use of Whippets, which could be let loose on the master's land, whereas the poacher, if he ventured there, could well be caught in a man trap or even shot.

Figs. 1806/1807
A pair of standing figures of a man and woman in Highland attire, he is wearing a plumed hat, his right hand holding a rifle, his left resting on his hip, a dog seated to his left, a dead bird to his feet, she with her right hand resting on the dog's head, her left arm across her waist, a dog seated to her right.
HEIGHT: 8.75 inches
PRICE: Pair: E, Singles: F.

Fig. 1808
A figure of a kilted Scotsman standing, wearing a short jacket, plumed hat, and cloak, his dog is begging to his left with its paws on the man's leg, to his right, his rifle stands against a tree stump.
This figure is usually found sparsely coloured, it is very rare to find it as illustrated. A version of this figure was found titled 'Mary Taylor' in gilt script and was ascribed to being a portrait of Mary Talbot who under the pseudonym 'John Taylor', after many adventures joined The Royal Navy and was wounded in action, and subsequently discharged without her true sex being discovered.
Another figure of a standing Greyhound has also been recorded titled 'Elizabeth Travis', no record of any such Greyhound can be found.
A much more likely and convincing explanation of 'titled' figures such as these is that they were titled by the potter and given to children of that name as presents.
HEIGHT: 14.25 inches
PRICE: Coloured: E, White: F.

Fig. 1808A
A figure of a bearded, kilted Scotsman standing wearing a short jacket, plumed hat, frilled shirt, and an ermine edged cloak over his left shoulder. His dog is begging to his left with its paws on the man's leg. To his right his rifle stands against a tree stump. He is holding a hare by its hind legs and a rabbit and bird lay on the base.
This is an altogether superior version of Fig. 1808. The basic model is the same but additional moulds have been added. A very rare version, the figure illustrated is the only example the authors have seen.
HEIGHT: 14 inches
PRICE: D.

Figs. 1809/1809A
A pair of spill vase group figures of huntsmen standing on scrolled, gilt lined bases, they are both dressed similarly with plumed hats, short jackets, long cloaks, boots, and pantaloons. One holds a long bow in his right hand and his dog sits at his feet. The other figure has his legs crossed and holds a deer suspended by its hind legs.
HEIGHT: 13 inches
PRICE: Pair: D, Singles: E.

Fig. 1810
A spill vase figure of a man standing on a coloured base, wearing a jacket, waistcoat, hat, and trousers with leggings, holding a rifle by the barrel in his right hand, his dog seated to his left, his hand on its head, a dead bird lies at his feet, behind him there is a large tree trunk, and a stile is attached to the tree.
Two figures illustrated. This figure is modelled in the round and a number of separate moulds would have been needed to complete this figure, the green and brown combing on the base is also indicative of this figure having been produced by The Parr factory, even though the colouring on the man's clothing varies, the base and spill vase palette stays the same.
HEIGHT: 13.5 inches
PRICE: E.

Figs. 1810A/1810B
A pair of figures of a huntsman and wife standing, both wear plumed hats. She has a blouse and long skirt, and holds a basket of fruit in her left hand, her right is on the head of a dog that stands on her right. He wears a long jacket and a sash over his shoulder supporting a bag. His right hand is held aloft holding a hunting horn and his left holds his rifle by its barrel with the butt on the ground. His dog stands beside him.
These figures are modelled and decorated in the round. A number of separate moulds were needed to complete the figures. They are early, made in the 1840s. Whilst the original maker is not known, sometime late in the century the moulds were acquired by The Kent factory and later figures made.
HEIGHT: 7.5 inches
PRICE: Pair: D, Singles: E.

Fig. 1811
A figure of a man standing on a coloured base, wearing a long coat, waistcoat, trousers with leggings, and a cap, holding his rifle in both hands across his chest, over his shoulder and left arm are sacks. His dog is seated behind him and to his left with its paws on an outcrop. There is a dead game bird at his feet and a dead rabbit by his right leg.
HEIGHT: 13 inches
PRICE: E.

Fig. 1812
A spill vase figure of a man standing, wearing a top hat, short coat, waistcoat, and trousers, a scarf flows over his right shoulder and through his left arm, holding his rifle in his left hand by the barrel with the butt on the ground. Behind him and to his right there is a tree stump, to his right are his two dogs, one seated and one standing.
HEIGHT: 11 inches
PRICE: D.

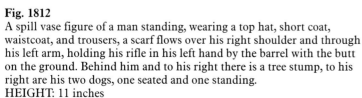

Fig. 1812A
A figure of a standing hunter with long hair and wearing a cap, belted tunic, breeches, knee boots, and a jumper tied by its sleeves over his shoulders. A shot bag is suspended from his shoulder. He is holding a rifle by its stock and barrel in both hands. His dog stands at his feet.
HEIGHT: 14 inches
PRICE: F.

Fig. 1812B
A figure of a hunter standing with one foot raised above the other on rock-work, he wears a hat with a plume, ermine edged cloak, jacket, frilled shirt, knee breeches, and boots. His right arm rests on rock-work, his right hand holding the barrel of his rifle, the butt of which rests on the ground. His dog sits at attention at his side.
HEIGHT: 13 inches
PRICE: F.

Fig. 1812C
A figure of a hunter standing, he wears a plumed hat, ermine edged cloak, short belted jacket, knee breeches, and boots. A small deer is held over his right shoulder and his left hand holds the barrel of his gun, with its butt on the ground. His dog sits to attention by his feet.
HEIGHT: 10 inches
PRICE: E.

Fig. 1813
A group figure of a huntsman standing, wearing Scottish apparel, including a sporran, holding a hunting horn to his mouth, his rifle in his left hand, behind and to his left his dog is on its hind legs with its paws on the man's side, a dead deer lies below.
HEIGHT: 13 inches
PRICE: E.

Fig. 1814
A group figure of a huntsman standing, dressed similarly to Figure 1813, however there are differences, the scarf is larger and more elaborate. The dog is posed differently and the deer is facing the other way, having a separately modelled head. **Altogether this is a finer, larger, and more elaborate version.**
HEIGHT: 14 inches
PRICE: E.

Fig. 1814A
A figure of a man standing with a dog, the dog is on its hind legs, its front paws resting on rock-work. The man, with his right arm raised to his head holding a horn and his left resting on his hip, wears a headscarf, tunic, pantaloons, and a large scarf across his shoulders and over his arms.
This figure has been included with hunters as he is holding what could be a hunting horn and has a dog; but, there is no gun or bow. It is likely, in view of his attire, that this figure actually represents a fairground entertainer or 'Barker' who played music and shouted to attract the attention of a crowd.
HEIGHT: 14.5 inches
PRICE: E.

Fig. 1815
A figure of a man standing, wearing a cap, long coat, waistcoat, and trousers with leggings, a scarf is over his shoulder and he carries a game bag, holding his rifle by the barrel in his left hand, he is muzzle loading it, his dog leaps to his left, there is a small stump behind him.
HEIGHT: 15 inches
PRICE: E.

Fig. 1817
A figure of a kilted Scotsman seated cross-legged on a shaped gilt lined base, wearing a plumed hat with a scarf over his right shoulder, from which two rabbits are suspended, holding a bird aloft in his left hand, his right hand holding his rifle by its barrel, his dog seated behind him and to his left.
HEIGHT: 15 inches
PRICE: E.

Fig. 1816
A figure of a man standing, wearing a plumed hat, tunic, and kilt with sporran, a large scarf over his shoulders and down his right side, holding his rifle in his right hand, his left held aloft holding a dead bird. His dog is on its hind legs with its paws on the man's kilt.
HEIGHT: 11 inches
PRICE: E.

Fig. 1817A
A figure of a hunter standing cross-legged with his dog seated at his feet, his right hand resting on rock-work, his left to his waist holding a rifle by its barrel, wearing a brimmed hat, head-scarf, shirt, and breeches.
HEIGHT: 10.25 inches
PRICE: E.

Fig. 1817C
A standing figure of a hunter wearing highland attire, he has a bag on his side suspended by a strap over his left shoulder. His right hand holds a lead to which is attached a dog, which sits between his legs. A weapon is held in his right hand.
HEIGHT: 12 inches
PRICE: F.

Fig. 1818
A figure of a man standing, wearing a plumed hat, waistcoat with tassels, long cloak, boots, and pantaloons, there is a horn in his waistband and he is holding a bird, probably a falcon, aloft in his left hand, his dog seated behind him and to his right.
HEIGHT: 15 inches
PRICE: E.

Fig. 1819
A figure of a man standing, wearing a long cap and cloak, tasselled jacket, pantaloons, and boots, holding a rifle by the barrel in his left hand, his right hand is on his hip, his dog seated to his right, a dead bird is by his rifle.
HEIGHT: 14.25 inches
PRICE: E.

Fig. 1820
A spill vase figure of a man standing on an arched scrolled gilt lined base, wearing a large plumed hat, short jacket, long cloak, pantaloons, and boots, holding a spear in his right hand, a dog seated to his right.
This figure is somewhat of an anomaly as on the base within the scroll there is often found the letters 'O R' in capitals, there has been much speculation what this means, but to date there has been no satisfactory answer.
This figure can be found in three sizes, 17 inch, which is usually a debased version with fewer mouldings, and 18 inch illustrated, and a superb 20 inch version which is rarely seen.
HEIGHT: 17 inches, Price: G, 18 inches, Price: F, 20 inches, Price: E.

Fig. 1821
A figure of a man standing, wearing a plumed hat, short cloak, jacket, and thigh boots, over his shoulder is a quiver, on his waist a horn, there is a long bow to his right, a dog stands on its hind legs with its paws in the man's right hand, his left hand is around the dog's shoulders.
HEIGHT: 13 inches
PRICE: E.

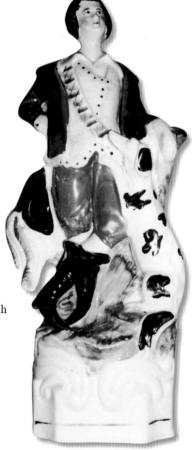

Fig. 1821A
A figure of a man standing with his legs crossed, wearing a short jacket, shirt, waistcoat with sash, knee breeches, and boots, holding his plumed hat in his right hand. His left hand rests on rock-work to his side. A dog stands on its hind legs with its forepaws on his leg, on a shaped and scrolled base.
This is a very rare figure and its pair is unrecorded. Fig. 1821B has been reserved for it. This appears to be a hunter, but no weapon is in evidence. Should the pair come to light, exactly what the figure represents may be resolved.
HEIGHT: 10.5 inches
PRICE: E.

Fig. 1822
A figure of a man seated on a grassy bank, wearing a long jacket, trousers with leggings, his left hand holding his rifle by the barrel, his right holding a bird aloft, a dog is to his right on its hind legs with its paws on the man's thigh.
HEIGHT: 12 inches
PRICE: E.

Fig. 1823/1824
A figure of a kilted man standing with plumed hat, short jacket, and cloak, holding his rifle in the crook of his right arm, his left hand is on his hip, a dog stands on its hind legs with its paws on his thigh, a dead bird lies at his feet, there is a large tree stump behind.
There are two versions of this figure illustrated, at first glance they appear the same but closer examination shows marked differences, the dog is finer and the bird and spill better modelled, one is very fine, the other superb, and it is these differences in quality which make the difference in price.
HEIGHT: 14 inches, Price: D, Fig 1823; 14 inches, Price: E, Fig 1824.

Far left:
Fig. 1824A
A spill vase figure of a hunter standing with his dog leaping up. The man's right hand is resting on his hip and his left raised to his chest holding a rifle in the crook of his arm. He is wearing a plumed hat, jacket, ermine edged cape, kilt, and boots. A dead bird is lying at his feet.
This figure is a reversed smaller version of Figures 1823/ 1824. It can be found in two sizes. The 9-inch version is illustrated.
HEIGHT: 9 inches and 13 inches
PRICE: 9-inch: F, 13-inch: E.

Left:
Fig. 1824B
A spill vase figure of a hunter standing with his dog leaping up at his side. The hunter's left hand rests on his hip and his right is raised to his chest holding a rifle in the crook of his arm. He wears a plumed hat, jacket, ermine edged cape, kilt, and boots. A dead bird is lying at his feet.
This figure is a smaller version of Figures 1823/1824.
HEIGHT: 9 inches
PRICE: F.

Fig. 1824D
A spill vase figure of a hunter seated, wearing a plumed hat, shirt, waistcoat, long jacket, and knee breeches. His left hand is in his jacket pocket and his right arm around his dog, which is to his right and is on its rear legs with its front paws in his lap. A rifle is also in his lap and at his feet lies a dead bird.
Two figures are illustrated. The dog has gone from black to red; apart from this they are virtually identical.
HEIGHT: 9 inches
PRICE: F.

Fig. 1824E
A spill vase figure of a hunter standing, wearing a plumed hat, ermine edged cloak, short jacket, shirt, kilt, and boots with short stockings. His right hand rests on his hip and his left holds his rifle. His dog stands on its hind legs with its forepaws on his knee. A dead bird lies on the base.
HEIGHT: 13.5 inches
PRICE: E.

Fig. 1825A
A spill vase figure of a standing Scotsman dressed in highland attire, a large tartan scarf is across his shoulder and over his left arm. One hand is on his hip and his right hand rests on the head of a dog that stands on its hind legs with its front paws on his kilt. Whilst no weapon is evident, the authors are of the opinion that this represents a hunter with his dog.
HEIGHT: 9 inches
PRICE: F.

Fig. 1825
A figure of a man standing, wearing a plumed hat, long coat, waistcoat, trousers with leggings, and boots, holding a rabbit in his left hand, another by his right, a brace of birds hang from a stump to his right, a rifle lies on the ground and a dog is seated on a mound to his left.
This figure can be found in two sizes.
HEIGHT: 13 inches, 15 inches
PRICE: E.

Fig. 1825C
A watch holder figure of a standing huntsman, his left arm leans on a closed spill vase in the form of a tree trunk. He wears a plumed hat, shirt, waistcoat, long jacket, and knee breeches. His rifle rests against the tree. Hanging from its branches are a dead bird and rabbit. His dog sits below the tree.
It is rare to find figures that are both a spill vase and a watch holder; it is not known why the spill was sometimes closed.
HEIGHT: 10.5 inches
PRICE: E.

Fig. 1826
A figure of a man seated cross-legged on a rocky mound, wearing a tricorn hat, jacket, waistcoat, and trousers with leggings, his right hand holding a rifle, his left around a dog seated to his left, there is a dead rabbit between his legs.
HEIGHT: 10 inches
PRICE: E.

Fig. 1827
A figure of a man standing, wearing a round cap, jacket, waistcoat, and trousers, right hand holding a rifle by the barrel, a dog seated between his legs.
By its composition and size, there is very likely a pair to this figure.
HEIGHT: 9 inches
PRICE: F.

Fig. 1828
A figure of a man standing cross-legged, wearing a plumed hat, short jacket, and pantaloons, a sash around his waist, his left hand holding a rifle by the barrel with the butt on the ground, a dog seated by his right leg, a dead bird by the rifle.
There is very likely a pair to this figure.
HEIGHT: 9.75 inches
PRICE: G.

Fig. 1828A
A spill vase figure of a huntsman standing with his dog seated at his feet, his right arm to his side holding a rifle and his left raised to his shoulder holding a dead bird. He is wearing a plumed hat, scarf, jacket, shirt, kilt, and boots.
HEIGHT: 9.5 inches
PRICE: F.

Fig. 1828F
A figure of a huntsman standing by a small gate wears a cap, jacket, and knee breeches, with a bag is suspended from his shoulder. In front of the gate a dog stands.
This figure probably has a pair. Fig. 1828G has been reserved for it.
HEIGHT: 4 inches
PRICE: G.

Fig. 1830A
A figure of a huntsman standing with one foot raised on rock-work, his dog to his left side with its paws on his knee, a dead deer below, his right arm to his side holding a rifle by its barrel and his left resting on his leg. He is wearing a tasselled hat, jacket, shirt, kilt, pantaloons, a scarf around his shoulders, and a strap across his chest.
HEIGHT: 15 inches
PRICE: E.

Fig. 1831A
A figure of a hunter kneeling on the back of a stag, a dog seated to his side with his front paws on his waist, his right arm raised to his head holding a hunting horn and his left to his side holding the deer's antlers. He wears a plumed hat, tunic, kilt and sporran, and a scarf across his chest.
This figure can be found in two sizes, both illustrated.
HEIGHT: 13.5 inches, 15.5 inches
PRICE: E.

Fig. 1831B
A spill vase figure of a hunter seated with his right arm leaning against a tree and holding a rifle by its barrel. He is wearing highland attire of plumed hat, open necked shirt, jerkin, kilt, and boots. A large scarf is over his left shoulder and across his chest. To his left a spaniel lays recumbent on rock-work and he rests his left hand on the spaniel's head. At his feet two birds lay dead.
HEIGHT: 14 inches
PRICE: D.

Fig. 1831D
A seated figure of a hunter wearing highland attire of cap, jacket with scarf, kilt with sporran, and shoes and socks. He rests his left arm on rock-work and his rifle is by his side with its stock on the ground. By his feet his dog sits.
HEIGHT: 12.5 inches
PRICE: E.

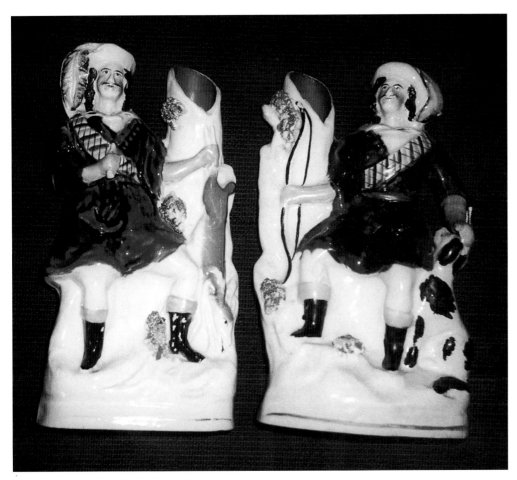

Figs. 1835C/1835D
A pair of spill vase figures of
standing huntsmen, both wear
similar clothes of plumed hat,
long tunic with a scarf across
their chest, and boots. The left
hand side figure holds a knife in
his right hand and a deer by its
hind legs in his left. The right
hand side figure holds a long
bow in his right hand and his left
rests on the head of a dog that
sits by his feet.
HEIGHT: 8.5 inches
PRICE: Pair: E, Singles: F.

Far left:
Fig. 1842
A figure of a man striding,
wearing Greco-Roman type
clothes with a plumed helmet
and a large scarf which is
billowing out behind him,
alongside and behind him is a
stag which he holds by its horns,
a dog is to the foreground
running alongside.
**A very detailed figure which
required a considerable number
of separate moulds and would
have been expensive to
produce.**
HEIGHT: 15 inches
PRICE: D.

Left:
Fig. 1843
A spill vase figure of a hunter
standing, wearing a plumed hat,
shirt, short coat, scarf, and kilt,
his right hand holding a rifle, a
dog seated against the base of the
tree with a dead bird at its feet.
HEIGHT: 16 inches
PRICE: F.

Fig. 1843A

A figure of a huntsman kneeling on rock-work on a rococo style base, a dog is seated to his right, his left hand is raised to his head holding a dead deer by its hind legs while his right hand rests on the dog's head. The huntsman is wearing a plumed hat, tunic, and kilt with sporran while a scarf is draped over his shoulder and across his chest.

HEIGHT: 11.5 inches

PRICE: E.

Fig. 1843B

A spill vase figure of a standing hunter holding his rifle vertically by the breech, his dog sits at his feet and below a large bird lays dead. He wears a turban with two large feathers, shirt, open jacket, kilt, boots, and a cape over one shoulder.

A superbly modelled and decorated figure, very rare, and similar to Fig 1843 other than minor modelling differences. This figure will always be more expensive than a mainly white figure due to the full colour decoration.

HEIGHT: 16 inches

PRICE: D.

Figs. 1848/1849
A pair of figures of male and female hunters, he is standing with one leg upon rock-work above the other, wearing a plumed hat, short jacket, and knee breeches, a scarf passed over one shoulder and through his arm, his left hand holding a rifle by the barrel, his right hand resting upon his knee, below him a stag lies at rest. She is standing, wearing a plumed hat, short coat and long skirt, a scarf over her shoulders and by her left side holding her rifle by the barrel in her right hand, her dog standing on its hind legs with its paws on her waist.
HEIGHT: Male: 13 inches,
Female: 12.5 inches
PRICE: Pair: D, Singles: E.

Fig. 1849A
A figure of a huntsman, his right leg raised and resting on rock-work, his left hand raised to his head holding a plumed hat while his right is to his waist holding a dead deer. A dog on its hind legs stands to his left with its paws resting on the man's kilt. The man is wearing a neckerchief, tunic, a kilt with a sporran, and a scarf over his shoulder.
A particularly fine example of a huntsman and very rare.
HEIGHT: 14 inches
PRICE: D.

Fig. 1852A
A group figure of a hunter and his wife standing side by side, he wearing a cap, neckerchief, long jacket, shirt, waistcoat, knee breeches, boots, and a strap across his right shoulder while holding his gun by the barrel with its butt on the ground; she wearing a plumed hat, bodice, and aproned skirt while holding a dead bird in her right hand. A spaniel lies recumbent between their feet.
HEIGHT: 10 inches
PRICE: E.

Figs. 1852B/1852C
A pair of spill vase figures of a standing hunter and wife, he wears a cap, waistcoat, jacket, trousers, and boots. His rifle is to his left with its butt on the ground. His left hand rests on his hip and his right on the tree below which his dogs sits. She wears a mop cap, scarf across her shoulders, bodice, and dress with an apron. She has a basket over her right arm in which there are dead rabbits. In her right hand she holds a dead bird by its feet. Another basket is at her feet.
These figures are representative of a successful hunt, the wife carrying the animals that her husband has shot.
HEIGHT: 11 inches
PRICE: Pair: E, Singles: F.

Fig. 1852D
A spill vase figure of a standing hunter. He is long-haired and bearded and wears a hat with feather, tunic, ermine-edged long cloak belted at the waist, and ankle boots. His left hand rests on his waist and his right holds a long bow. A dog sits at his feet and all rests on an arched base with a shell decoration.
There is a pair to this very large figure. 1852E has been reserved for it.
HEIGHT: 17 inches
PRICE: E

212

Figs. 1853/1854
A pair of figures of hunters standing,
both wearing plumed hats, long coats,
trousers, and knee boots, one holding
his rifle in his right hand and holding a
scarf, which is draped over his shoulder
with his left. His dog is behind his
right leg. His left hand holds a dead
stag by the feet, which is draped over
his left shoulder.
**It is unusual for a pair of standing
figures to be both men, unless they
are a mirror image.**
HEIGHT: 9.75 inches
PRICE: Pair: E, Singles: F.

Right:
Fig. 1854A
A figure of a standing huntsman with
his dog seated below. His left hand is
resting on his hip, holding a sheaf of
corn, his right is raised to his chest
holding a horn. He is wearing a plumed
hat, jacket, and kilt, with a sash over his
shoulder and across his waist.
**There is probably a pair to this
figure. Figure 1854B has been
reserved for it.**
**In view of the fact that he is holding
corn under his arm, it is possible that
he may not be a hunter. Should the
pair come to light, the question of
exactly what he represents could well
be resolved.**
HEIGHT: 8 inches
PRICE: Pair: F, Singles: F.

Far right:
Fig. 1855A
A figure of a man standing on a circular
gilt lined base, holding the barrel of a
rifle in his right hand, a dead bird in his
left. A dog is standing on its hind legs
with its front paws resting on his coat.
The man is wearing a brimmed hat,
long jacket, and breeches.
It is probable that there is a pair to this
figure; Figure 1855B has been reserved
for it.
HEIGHT: 6.5 inches
PRICE: F.

Figs. 1856/1857
A pair of figures of male and female falconers standing cross-legged, wearing plumed hats, he with short jacket, trousers, and knee boots, she with bodice and long dress, both hold the falcons on their arms, he on his right, she on her left, his left hand holding a rifle by the barrel, his dog standing on its hind legs with paws to his waist, she holding what appears to be a garland of flowers in her right hand, the significance of which is unknown. **Two pairs are illustrated, as an example of incorrect restoration, the man should be holding a falcon, at some stage his arm was lost, not having an example from which to copy the restorer has not replaced the missing bird, this would affect the price, and the figure needs to be restored correctly.**
HEIGHT: 13 inches
PRICE: Pair: D, Singles: F.

Figs. 1858/1859
A pair of figures of a hunter and his wife, both standing on rock-work, wearing wide brimmed hats, he with short jacket, waistcoat, knee length trousers, leggings, and shoes, his right hand holding the barrel of his rifle, his left around his dog which is standing on its hind legs with its paws on his knees. Over his right shoulder there hangs a dead rabbit. She is wearing a short bodice, long dress with apron, holding a basket by both hands on her left hip. **These figures are modelled in the round and are products of The Parr factory.**
HEIGHT: 12 inches
PRICE: Pair: E, Singles: F.

Figs. 1860/1861
A pair of figures of a Scottish huntsman and wife standing on circular gilt lined bases, he is wearing typical highland garb of a feathered hat, tunic, kilt, and sporran, holding his rifle under his right arm, she is wearing a plumed hat, bodice, and long dress, both have their dogs standing on its hind legs with paws on their waists.
These figures are modelled in the round and are a matched pair, the base of one is coloured and the other is not, it is highly unlikely that they would have left the factory so mis-matched.
HEIGHT: 7.5 inches
PRICE: Pair: E, Singles: F.

Figs. 1862/1863
A pair of figures of a huntsman and wife standing, he has a large peaked hat, long jacket, waistcoat, knee length trousers, and ankle boots, a large scarf over his right shoulder and through his right arm, holding his rifle by the barrel in his left hand against his side, his dog which is to his right standing on its hind legs with its paws on his knees. She is wearing a bonnet tied with ribbon, short bodice and long dress, a scarf over her right arm, her right hand holding a dead rabbit, with her left holding a basket containing dead birds, her dog seated to her left on rock-work.
HEIGHT: 11.5 inches
PRICE: Pair: E, Singles: F.

Figs. 1864/1865
A very large and imposing pair of figures of a Tyrolean hunter and wife, both standing on rock-work, he is wearing a steepled brimmed hat, short jacket, waistcoat, knee length trousers, and socks, his left hand holding a rifle by the barrel, his right hand resting on rock-work, his dog seated at his feet. She is wearing a brimmed hat, short bodice, long dress with apron, holding a small dog to her waist.
These figures are modelled in the round, and are the product of The Parr factory.
HEIGHT: 16.75 inches
PRICE: Pair: D, Singles: F.

215

Fig. 1866
A spill vase group figure of two hunters and their dog, standing either side of a tree trunk, both wearing plumed hats, tunic, and skirt with thigh boots, on their waists hang hunting horns, to either side they hold a longbow, a large dog seated between.
These figures are invariably wearing a Lincoln green, and it has been suggested that they represent Robin Hood and Little John, however no titled figure is known to exist. A smaller 6-inch version exists which is of little quality.
HEIGHT: 12 inches
PRICE: F.

Figs. 1866A
A spill vase figure of a standing hunter, he is dressed in a plumed hat, belted tunic with straps, boots, and a hunting horn at his waist. He leans against the spill vase holding a club in his left hand. His dog sits on the other side of the spill vase.
HEIGHT: 12.25 inches
PRICE: F.

Figs. 1866C/1866D
A pair of spill vase figures of standing hunters, both are wearing plumed hats, belted tunics with straps across their chests, and a hunting horn at their belts. One stands beside a tree trunk holding a large club in his left hand and his right hand is on his hip holding a dead deer by its hind legs. His companion has his left hand on his hip and his right holds a long bow. A dog sits at his feet.
These two particular gentlemen do appear as a pair or in a group in a number of figures. They have never been found titled but do no doubt represent a particular pair of individuals, as yet unidentified. This pair are by far the rarest, largest, and finest of the figures.
HEIGHT: 16.5 inches
PRICE: Pair: D, Singles: F.

Fig. 1866E
A standing figure of a man dressed in highland attire of plumed hat, ermine edged cloak and jerkin, kilt, and ankle boots. He holds a long bow in his right hand and a dog sits by his left leg.
This is a very rare figure the authors have not seen it before. There is no doubt a pair and 1866F has been reserved for it.
HEIGHT: 8.75 inches
PRICE: F.

Figs. 1867/1868
A pair of figures of hunters standing on coloured arched bases, both wearing plumed hats, long jackets, and boots, one holding a long bow in his right hand, the other holding a large club in his left hand, his dog seated by his right leg.
These figures are modelled in the manner of The Parr factory.
HEIGHT: 11.5 inches
PRICE: Pair: F, Singles: G.

Figs. 1869/1870
A pair of figures of huntsmen standing, wearing plumed hats, long jackets, and boots, one holding a dead stag aloft by its feet in his left hand, his long bow rests against his arm, his right hand resting on his hip, the other holding a crossbow in his left hand, his right hand resting on his hip, his dog seated below by his right leg.
HEIGHT: 9 inches
PRICE: Pair: F, Singles: G.

Figs. 1872A/1872B
A pair of figures of a man and a woman on horseback with a dog standing on its hind legs below, on gilt lined rococo style bases. He, holding the dog's nose with his right hand while his left is holding the horse's mane, wears a plumed hat, long coat, and scarf. She, with her left hand holding the dog's nose and her right holding the horse's mane, wears a plumed hat, bodice, long dress, and a scarf around her chest.
HEIGHT: 8.25 inches
PRICE: Pair: E, Singles: F.

Figs. 1877
A watch-holder group figure of standing falconers, she to the left wearing a short bodice and long dress, he is standing to the right wearing a highland attire of long sleeved tunic, kilt and socks, a dog seated on its hind legs between them with its paws on the man's kilt, they both hold a bird aloft.
The master's pocket watch served two purposes, when he was out, it resided in his waistcoat pocket, when at home it was placed in the watch-holder, on the mantel-piece.
HEIGHT: 12.5 inches
PRICE: F

Figs. 1880/1881
A pair of figures of seated falconers, he wears a plumed hat, cloak, jacket, waistcoat, and knee breeches, and holds a falcon aloft in his left hand. His right hand rests on his knee. His dog is recumbent at his feet. She wears a plumed hat, wide sleeved blouse, and long dress. She holds the falcon aloft in her left hand. Her dog has leaped onto her lap. All rest on a shaped base decorated with gold sprays.
HEIGHT: 15 inches
PRICE: E.

Fig. 1893C

A figure of a woman standing on rock-work wearing a plumed hat, blouse with sash over her shoulder and across her chest, and a skirt with an apron. She also appears to have a full quiver on her back. To her left side also resting on rock-work is a basket filled with dead birds. On the base below her stands a spaniel.

This figure is no doubt one of a pair. Fig. 1893D has been reserved for it. This is an attractive figure that the authors have not seen before. Should the pair come to light, it probably portrays a hunter responsible for the dead birds.

HEIGHT: 9.75 inches

PRICE: F.

Figs. 1893E/1893F

A pair of figures of a man and woman standing, he wears a hat, frilled shirt with tie, jacket, and knee breeches. Over his shoulder is the strap of a bag, which he holds at his waist. His right hand holds the barrel of his gun with its butt on the ground. A dead bird is suspended from his right hand and his dog sits to attention at his feet. She wears a hat, bodice, jacket, and long skirt with an apron. There are two dead birds suspended from her left arm and her dog sits to attention at her feet. Both figures are on scrolled bases.

A particularly fine pair of hunters and very rare.

HEIGHT: 10.75 inches

PRICE: Pair: D, Singles: E.

Figs. 1893G/1893H

A pair of figures of a man and woman standing, he wears a hat with feathers, open neck shirt with tie, long jacket, knee length breeches and boots, and a sash across his chest. His left hand is in his jacket pocket and his right holds a rifle by its barrel. A dog sits at his feet. She wears a hat with feathers, long jacket, and a dress. She has a long scarf over her arm.

These figures were made by the Sampson Smith pottery circa 1860. In 1949 a mould of her was found in a disused part of the factory and a number of figures were then made and care should be taken as both the 1860 and 1949 figures were very similarly decorated.

HEIGHT: 10.25 inches

PRICE: Pair: E, Singles: G.

Fig. 1894
A figure of a man standing, wearing a plumed hat, split jacket, frilled shirt, knee length trousers, and boots, a scarf is over his shoulders, a bird seated on his right shoulder and holding a round garland to his left shoulder. There is rock-work to his right and his dog is seated at his feet. The origin of this figure is almost certainly theatrical, and there is more than likely a pair.
HEIGHT: 12 inches
PRICE: F.

Fig. 1898D
A standing figure of a woman dressed in a plumed hat, blouse, bodice, and long skirt with a scarf over her arm. She holds a dead bird aloft. A dog sits on rock-work to her right with its paws on her skirt.
HEIGHT: 12 inches
PRICE: Pair: D, Singles: E.

Fig. 1900
A group figure of a standing man and seated woman, he is wearing a plumed hat, long jacket, long waistcoat, knee length trousers and stockings. He has a cloak over his shoulder. She is seated wearing a head-dress with scarf, open-sleeved blouse, and long dress. A dog is seated at his feet and a bird is held on his right hand.
HEIGHT: 13 inches
PRICE: F.

Fig. 1902B
A group clock face figure of a hunter standing wearing a plumed hat, frilled shirt, jacket, and knee breeches with boots, holding a rifle by its butt in his right hand and his left is around a large dog that sits above the clock face. To the right, a woman sits wearing a plumed hat, bodice, long coat, and dress. Her hands are in her lap and at her feet lay a dead bird and rabbit.
HEIGHT: 12.5 inches
PRICE: E.

Fig. 1912
A figure of a standing boar hunter, wearing a plumed hat, jacket, knee length trousers, and boots, a large scarf over his shoulder and through his arm, a wide belt around his waist, holding his spear in his left hand and a hunting horn in his right, a foot resting on the dead boar, his dog seated between his legs and laying on the boar.
One of the tallest and most impressive figures to have come out of the potteries.
HEIGHT: 19 inches
PRICE: C.

Fig. 1913
A spill vase figure of a standing otter hunter, wearing a plumed hat, long jacket, and waistcoat, pleated shirt, short trousers with stockings and boots, his left hand is on his hip, his right holding a spear on which an otter is impaled. On the base are two otter hounds, one on its hind legs, the other laying between his feet. There is a large tree trunk behind which forms the spill.
HEIGHT: 16.5 inches
PRICE: D.

Fig. 1913B
A spill vase group figure of a man wearing a plumed hat, cloak, frilled shirt, and kilt with boots, holding a bird aloft with his right hand and his left is at his waist. To his right, a child sits in a tree with its hand reaching up to the bird; below a dog sits. **A very large and imposing figure and very rare, the figure illustrated is the only example the authors have seen.** HEIGHT: 16.5 inches PRICE: E.

Fig. 1914
A spill vase group figure of a rabbit catcher, kneeling beside a burrow, wearing a hat, long coat, knee breeches, and boots, the burrow is netted and his dog seated to his left, his right hand holding one rabbit, another lays on the ground by the burrow. There is a large tree trunk to his left on which he rests his arm. HEIGHT: 8.75 inches PRICE: F.

Fig. 1914A
A spill vase group figure of a man kneeling beside a tree trunk, his right hand raised holding a brimmed hat, wearing a jacket, neckerchief, waistcoat, and breeches. A dog chases a stag below.
This figure is a product of the 'Green' factory/modeller. HEIGHT: 8.5 inches PRICE: E.

Fig. 1914B
A spill vase group figure of a man seated wearing a
brimmed hat, cravat, shirt, jacket, and trousers with
leggings holding a rifle by its barrel between his legs.
A dog lies at his feet.
HEIGHT: 7 inches
PRICE: F.

Fig. 1914D
A spill vase group of a kneeling man wearing a hat,
jacket, shirt with tie, waistcoat, knee breeches, and
boots. One dog is to his left side with its forepaws on
his lap, another is by his left hand, and yet another
lies below. On the base is his rifle and a dead rabbit.
HEIGHT: 7.5 inches
PRICE: F.

Figs. 1916A/1916B
A pair of figures of a standing girl and boy with spaniels
standing to their sides. The girl, with her right arm
raised holding a dead rabbit and her left to her side,
wears a plumed hat, jacket, blouse, and an aproned skirt;
the boy, with his left arm raised holding a dead rabbit
and his right to his side, wears a plumed hat, shirt,
jacket, a kilt with sporran, and a sash across his chest.
HEIGHT: 9.5 inches
PRICE: Pair: F, Singles: G.

Figs. 1917/1918/1919

Three figures of archers standing, all similar but with differences. The first archer has a flat cap, a belt across his chest, two separately moulded arms, and the bow is also separately moulded. The second archer has a plumed hat, no belt, and the bow and one arm are not separately modelled. The third archer has a larger hat and bow. The dog remains the same in all three figures.

It is interesting that the potters should have made these changes; the second and third figures required fewer moulds and were therefore less work to produce. Why the figure was altered again is not known.
HEIGHT: 8.75 inches
PRICE: F.

Figs. 1920A/1920B

A pair of figures of huntsmen with dogs. The huntsman to the left, standing cross-legged with a bow in his right hand, wears a plumed hat, long tunic, boots, and a sash around his chest. A dog is leaping to his side. The man to the right is similarly attired, his right hand resting on his hip and his left to his side holding a horn. A dog stands by his right leg.
HEIGHT: 8.25 inches
PRICE: Pair: F, Singles: G.

Figs. 1921A/1921B
A pair of spill vase figures of a man and girl standing, the man with a dog standing over dead birds to his left. His right hand is resting on his hip, his left to his side holding a rifle with the butt on the ground, wearing a brimmed hat, jacket, shirt, and breeches, with a sash around his waist. The girl with a turkey standing to her side eating from a bowl, her left hand resting on her hip, her right resting on the turkey's head, wearing a head-scarf blouse, bodice, and long dress.
It is probable that these figures represent a farmer and wife, he with his shotgun.
HEIGHT: 12 inches
PRICE: Pair: E, Singles: F.

Fig. 1924
A spill vase group figure of two children, he is standing to the left holding a dead rabbit aloft, wearing a highland garb of feathered hat, tunic, kilt, sporran, and socks. She is seated on a fence to the right. A dog stands below, looking at the rabbit. Behind them is a large tree trunk.
HEIGHT: 11.5 inches
PRICE: F.

Fig. 1924B
A spill vase group of a hunter and his wife, he wears a flat cap, long jacket, flowered waistcoat, and knee breeches with boots. He holds his rifle by its barrel in his right hand and his left is around his wife. His wife is bareheaded and wears a bodice, long skirt with an apron, her hat is held in her right hand, and a filled basket is over her left arm. A small picket fence is by her feet and a dog sits by his master. The spill is decorated with grapes and a vine leaf.
HEIGHT: 16 inches
PRICE: E.

Figs. 1925/1926
A pair of figures of standing Scotsmen, both wearing highland garb of a plumed hat, tunic, shirt, kilt and sporran, one has his left hand resting on rock-work, his right hand holding a pistol that is pointed at a deer, which lays below. The other man stands legs astride, one higher than the other on rock-work, holding a pistol by its barrel. His dog stands between his legs.
HEIGHT: 7.5 inches
PRICE: Pair: E, Singles: F.

Fig. 1927
A group figure of a Scotsman, his wife, and child. He stands wearing highland garb of cap, tunic, shirt, kilt and socks, his dog by his legs. His wife is on the right wearing a plumed hat, bodice, and long dress. Between them they hold a child.
It has been suggested that this group represents 'The MacDonalds of Glencoe' and was once sold and described as 'A group figure of the MacDonalds of Glencoe, MacIan defending his wife and child from the Campbell's'. In view of Figure 1926, which is identical to the man in this figure, this description is unlikely.
HEIGHT: 12.5 inches
PRICE: F.

Figs. 1931A/1931B
A pair of figures of a man and woman standing with dogs to their sides. The man, holding a whip in his right hand and his left arm around the dog, wears a plumed hat, shirt, kilt and sporran, and a sash across his chest. The woman, with her right hand on the dog's neck, wears a plumed hat, blouse, skirt, and a sash across her chest.
HEIGHT: 7.5 inches
PRICE: Pair: E, Singles: F.

Figs. 1935A/1935B
A pair of figures of a man and a shepherdess, both
standing, he wearing a cap, jacket, scarf, and breeches
with leggings. His gun stands on its butt between his
legs and he is filling it with shot from a bag held in his
hand. His dog sits to his side. She wears a brimmed hat,
bodice, and skirt with an apron. She holds a sheep by its
neck and appears to be removing wool from it.
**These are early figures modelled in the round with a
number of separate moulds, made in about 1830/35.**
HEIGHT: 8 inches
PRICE: Pair: E, Singles: F.

Figs. 1935C/1935D
A pair of figures of a woman and man standing, she wears a mop
cap, blouse, and long skirt with an apron. She has her left hand
around a dog that stands on its hind legs at her side and she holds
a rabbit in her right hand. He wears a brimmed hat, shirt, long
jacket, and knee breeches. A pouch hangs at his side. He holds a
rifle by the barrel that has its stock on the ground and a dog
stands on its hind legs in front of him. He holds a dead bird in his
left hand.
**These are early figures modelled in the round with a
number of separate moulds, made in about 1830/35.**
HEIGHT: 7.25 inches
PRICE: Pair: E, Singles: F.

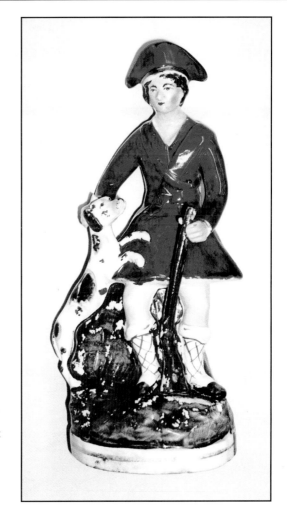

Fig. 1935E
A standing figure of a man wearing a tri-corn hat, long tunic, and
shoes and socks. His right hand rests on the head of a dog that
stands on its hind legs and his left holds the barrel of his rifle that
has its butt on the ground.
HEIGHT: 9 inches
PRICE: G.

Fig. 1943

An arbour group figure of a standing man attacking another, the man to the left holding a pistol and wearing a brimmed hat, long jacket, waistcoat, and trousers with leggings, the man to the right wearing top hat, long jacket, waistcoat, and trousers with leggings. A dog is also attacking the man on the right, although armed with a rifle he holds it by his side, there are two dead birds on the ground.

There has been speculation as to the inspiration for this group figure and it has for many years been described as being of William Smith and Thomas Collier, Collier being a tenant farmer, who was also a poacher, murdered Smith when he was caught in the act by him. This remains speculation and is not feasible, Smith was killed by a rifle, not clubbed by a pistol, there was no mention of a dog, and a titled figure has never been found to exist. Finally this murder took place in 1866, and this and the next three figures date to the early 1850s.

As can be seen from this and the next three figures, this was a popular theme and, whilst representing a quarrel, its origin is either theatrical or another print.

HEIGHT: 13.25 inches

PRICE: E.

Figs. 1944

Another superior spill vase version of the Figure 1943, the man on the left wearing a bowler hat, long jacket, waistcoat, and trousers with leggins, holding his pistol by the barrel as though to club his opponent, his dog leaps at the other man's throat, who is bareheaded, wearing a long coat, waistcoat, and trousers with leggings, he supports himself on a tree stump. On the ground there lies a rifle and a dead bird, to the rear is a large tree stump which forms the spill.

See comments on Figure 1943. This no doubt represents a gamekeeper/ poacher argument, but not Smith and Collier.

Two figures shown, identical apart from the spill, one is open the other is closed.

HEIGHT: 14 inches

PRICE: D.

Fig. 1945

A very rare spill vase version of Figures 1943/1944, the man on the left wearing a top hat, neckerchief, long jacket, waistcoat, and trousers with leggings, being clubbed by a pistol held by the man on the right who is similarly dressed but is bareheaded, once again the dog attacks the man wearing the top hat, and whilst there are dead birds on the ground, there is no rifle. There is a tree trunk which forms the spill at the back.

HEIGHT: 9.75 inches

PRICE: D.

Figures 1949 to 1956 all depict fox or stag hunting, a sport that has recently been banned in England. This is a 300-year-old tradition that has fallen foul of politically correct opinion that has little knowledge or regard for the countryside. Now foxes will be shot, leaving many suffering from injuries that will leave them a lingering death.

Dogs have served Shepherds for centuries. Without his sheepdog, a shepherd's life would have been almost impossible. He was a servant, companion, pet, and many were guard dogs as well.

Figs. 1949/1950
A very fine pair of equestrian huntsmen, they are mirror images of each other. They sit astride their horses holding the reins in one hand and a hunting horn in the other. Both huntsmen wear a cap, long jacket, and trousers with boots. Below them the hunt is taking place with a dog, which has leaped onto the back of a stag.
HEIGHT: 11 inches
PRICES: Pair: C, Singles: E.

Figs. 1950A/1950B
A pair of figures of equestrian huntsmen facing left and right, the horses rearing up with their front feet resting on a fence, and a dog chasing below. Both figures are dressed similarly, wearing a cap, buttoned tunic, breeches, and boots.
HEIGHT: 9 inches
PRICE: Pair: C, Singles: E.

Fig. 1952E
A spill vase figure of a hunter seated wearing a plumed hat, shirt, cloak, and kilt with boots, holding a pail in both hands from which his horse is drinking. Over the saddle of the horse, a dead bird and rabbit lay and below a dog is recumbent.
HEIGHT: 12 inches
PRICE: E.

Figs. 1953/1953A
'The Fox Hunt' is a well-constructed pair of groups of this subject, which can be found in two sizes, the huntsman seated astride his horse which is galloping, wearing hunting attire, below there are two dogs chasing a fox in one group and in the other they are chasing a rabbit.
HEIGHT: 7.5 & 10 inches
PRICE: 7.5 inch: F, 10 inch: E.

Figs. 1954/1955
A pair of figures of equestrian huntsmen, seated astride their horses similarly attired, one in top hat and one in cap, the left hand side figure holding a hunting horn in his right hand, below him lies a stag at rest. The right hand side figure's horse is prancing and below him runs his dog.
HEIGHT: 7 inches
PRICE: Pair: E, Singles: F.

Fig. 1956
A spill vase hunting group figure of a man astride his horse, wearing a cap, jacket, and trousers with boots with a large tree stump spill to his left, a small fence alongside, his dog standing below, and a stag is at rest below the fence.
This may well have been designed as a centrepiece to Figures 1954/1955 and all three are illustrated together.
HEIGHT: 8 inches
PRICE: E.

Right:
Fig. 1961A
A figure of a standing shepherd wearing a plumed hat, long jacket, shirt, waistcoat, and knee breeches with a cloak over his shoulder, his right hand on his hip and his left holds a crook. A sheep lies at his feet and, to his side on a rock, a Poodle sits with its paw on his shoulder.
A very rare group, it is also unusual to have a Poodle as a sheep dog!
HEIGHT: 13.5 inches
PRICE: D.

Far right:
Fig. 1961B
A figure of a highland shepherd standing with legs crossed, he wears a plumed hat, shirt, jacket, and kilt with boots, holding a sheep under his right arm. A water bottle and pipe are suspended from his waist. His dog sits at attention to his left side and another sheep lies on the base.
HEIGHT: 10.5 inches
PRICE: F.

Fig. 1962A
A figure of a standing shepherd, his dog seated to his right on a rock-work, a lamb standing on its hind legs with its front legs resting on his waist and another lamb lying below. The shepherd, his right hand on his hip holding a water flask and his left to his side with his hand resting on the lamb's shoulder, wears a brimmed hat, jacket, neckerchief, shirt, breeches, and stockings.
HEIGHT: 12 inches
PRICE: E.

Figs. 1965C/1965D
A pair of figures of standing shepherds, both wearing plumed hats, she a blouse, long coat, and long skirt, he a long jacket, shirt with tie, and knee breeches. She holds a lamb in her left arm and another lamb lies on the base, a small fence is to her right. He holds a dog under his right arm and two lambs lay on the base.
HEIGHT: 6.25 inches
PRICE: Pair: F, Singles: G.

Figs. 1967A/1967B
A pair of figures of a boy and girl, both standing on rock-work and wearing plumed hats, he with a shirt, jacket, and knee breeches with his right arm around a spaniel that stands on its hind legs beside him. She wears a bodice and long skirt, holding an apron that is filled with fruit. A lamb stands on rock-work to her side
HEIGHT: 8.5 inches
PRICE: Pair: E, Singles: F.

Figs. 1968A/1968
A pair of figures of a shepherd and shepherdess, both wearing highland attire of plumed hat, blouse/tunic with sash, and skirt/kilt, he with boots and she with shoes. He stands and holds a set of pipes in both hands. Below him a dog is recumbent; she sits cross-legged and holds an open book in both hands. At her feet sits a sheep.
The figure of the shepherdess is similar in some respects to a Pre-Victorian figure titled 'The Reading Maid' illiteracy being common it was a source of amazement that a young girl could read.
HEIGHT: 11 inches
PRICE: Pair D Singles E

Figs. 1968D/1968E
A pair of figures of highland shepherds, both standing, he wears a plumed hat, long tunic, tartan socks, and shoes. A large scarf is draped over his left shoulder. He holds a set of bagpipes in his left hand. Below him, on the base, his dog lays. She wears a plumed hat, long sleeved blouse, and long skirt. A large scarf is over her right shoulder and across her chest. A sheep stands on its hind legs to her side with its forepaws on her waist. Two lambs lie on the base.
HEIGHT: 11 inches
PRICE: Pair: E, Singles: F.

Fig. 1969
A spill vase figure of a shepherd standing, holding in his left hand a crook, his right holding pipes, wearing a wide brimmed hat, open necked shirt with kerchief, open waistcoat, and knee length breeches with ankle boots, to the right a dog is seated with one paw held up, a small sheep lay's below, to the back is a tree trunk.
HEIGHT: 10 inches
PRICE: F.

Fig. 1969E
A figure of a shepherd seated on rock-work, he wears a bonnet, shirt jacket, kilt, and long socks. A sash is over his shoulder and across his chest. He holds a crook in his right hand and his dog stands on its hind legs with its forepaws on his leg.
HEIGHT: 8.5 inches
PRICE: G.

Fig. 1970
A spill vase figure of a standing shepherdess, wearing a plumed hat, bodice, and long skirt, a large scarf around her neck and body, to the left a tree trunk with her crook resting against it, a dog lays below.
This may be a representation of the nursery rhyme 'Little Bo Peep', as there are no sheep to be seen.
HEIGHT: 10.75 inches
PRICE: E.

Fig. 1973H

A spill vase group figure of a shepherd and shepherdess, he standing and she seated leaning against a tree trunk. He wears a plumed hat, jacket, waistcoat, and knee breeches. His left foot is raised onto a mound and by his feet a dog sits and a sheep lies. She wears a hat, bodice, and long skirt and rests her head on her right hand.
HEIGHT: 10 inches
PRICE: F.

Fig. 1972

A figure of a standing shepherd, wearing a coat, shirt, and knee length trousers with leggings, holding his crook in front of him in both hands, to his right on the ground is his hat, his dog seated below. To his left his flock is seated in front of a small fence.
HEIGHT: 10 inches
PRICE: F.

Figs. 1973F/1973G

A pair of spill vase figures of a boy and girl seated, each wearing a hat, blouse, and skirt/kilt. A stream runs at their feet and a lamb stands to her side and a dog to his with its forepaws on his lap.
HEIGHT: 6 inches
PRICE: Pair: F, Singles: G.

Fig. 1973J

A watch holder group of a man and woman standing, both wearing plumed hats, he a tunic with sash across his chest, she wears a blouse and long skirt. At their feet a dog and sheep sit. Above them is an arbour covered in a fruiting grapevine.
HEIGHT: 9 inches
PRICE: G.

Fig. 1974

A group figure of a standing man and woman, she is to the left wearing a ribboned bonnet, bodice, and aproned dress, he to the right with ribboned hat, long coat, open necked shirt, waistcoat, and knee length trousers with tied socks. He has a barrel suspended from his left shoulder and there is a sheep around his neck. Between them there is a goat and below, seated, their dog.
HEIGHT: 12.5 inches
PRICE: E.

Figs. 1976A/1976B

A pair of spill vase figures of a girl and a boy, the spill decorated with a plant growing up it. The girl, with her right arm across her chest and her left to her side resting on the head of a lamb, which is standing on its hind legs, wears a plumed hat, bodice, skirt, and knickers. The boy, standing cross-legged, holding musical pipes, a dog to his side standing on its hind legs with its front paws on his coat, wears a plumed hat, neckerchief, shirt, long jacket, and trousers.
HEIGHT: 10 inches
PRICE: Pair: E, Singles: F.

Figs. 1976C/1976D

A pair of spill vase figures of a sleeping shepherd and shepherdess, both are laying down with their heads resting on the spill. He wears a hat, shirt, jacket, and trousers, she a hat, blouse, and long skirt. Their crooks rest on the spill and there is a dog at his feet and a sheep at hers.
HEIGHT: 5.5 inches
PRICE: Pair: F, Singles: G.

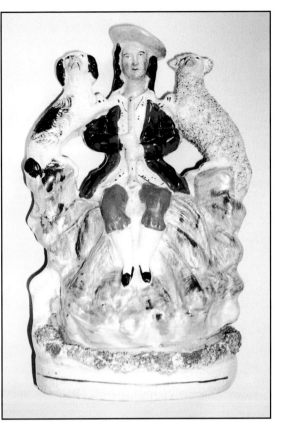

Fig. 1976E/1976F
A pair of groups of a shepherd and shepherdess, both seated on a grassy mound. He wears a bonnet, shirt, long jacket, and knee breeches. He holds pipes in both hands. Standing on their hind legs on either side is a dog and a sheep, each of which have their forepaws on the man's shoulders. She wears a hat, jacket, blouse, and skirt with an apron. To either side of her, a sheep stands with its forepaws on her shoulder. On the base below each figure a stream flows. **The figures illustrated are a matched pair and the figure of her has suffered substantial damage that has not been repaired.**
HEIGHT: 8 inches
PRICE: Pair: F, Singles: G.

Figs. 1977/1978
A pair of figures of a shepherd and shepherdess, both seated. He wears a hat, waistcoat, shirt with tie, and knee breeches. A sheep feeds from a bowl that is in his hand. She wears a brimmed hat and long dress. A large dog sits to her side and feeds from a bowl in her hand.
An almost identical figure of 1978 was made in Parian by Samuel Alcock & Co., circa 1840/1850. This figure also had a pair, but the pair to the Alcock figure is of another girl feeding a lamb, not a boy.
HEIGHT: 7 inches
PRICE: Pair: F, Singles: G.

Figs. 1979D/1979E
A pair of figures of a girl and boy standing on
rock-work. The girl, with a lamb to her right, is
holding a crook in her left hand and a scarf in
her right, which billows behind her. She is
wearing a plumed bonnet, bodice, and skirt.
The boy, with a dog seated to his left, is
holding a staff in his right hand and his left is
resting on his hip. He wears a plumed hat,
scarf, jacket, waistcoat, shirt, and breeches.
HEIGHT: 8 inches
PRICE: Pair: E, Singles: F.

Figs. 1981A/1981B
A pair of figures of a standing boy and a girl. The boy,
with a dog to his left, his right hand to his side
holding a crook and his left raised to his chest, wears a
brimmed hat, shirt, breeches, and a sash around his
waist. The girl, with a lamb to her right, her right arm
to her side and her left raised to her chest holding a
pipe, wears a headscarf, bodice, and an aproned dress.
HEIGHT: 9.5 inches
PRICE: Pair: F, Singles: G.

Figs. 1981C/1981D
A pair of figures of a boy and girl, he seated and she lying. The
children wear plumed hats, tunic/blouse, and kilt/skirt. The boy
holds a dog on his lap and the girl a sheep while below another
sheep is recumbent.
The small holes on the base are for use as quill holders.
HEIGHT: 4.75 inches
PRICE: Pair: F, Singles: G.

Figs. 1981E/1981F
A pair of figures of a boy and girl reclining with an elbow resting on rock-work, she is bareheaded and wears a blouse and long skirt. A sheep stands by her side with its forepaws on her lap. Her left arm rests on its back. He wears an open neck shirt, short jacket, kilt, and boots. A dog stands by his side with its forepaws on his lap. His right arm rests on its back.
The 'Alpha' factory made these figures, and the modeller used very similar heads on many of his figures, some of which portrayed The Royal Children.
HEIGHT: 5.5 inches
PRICE: Pair: F, Singles: G.

Figs. 1982C/1982D
A pair of spill vase standing figures of a girl and boy. The girl, holding a cat in her lap with a goat rearing on its hind legs to her right, wears a bodice and a long dress. The boy, resting against the trunk of the spill, his right hand in his coat pocket and his left resting on the head of his dog, which is seated at his feet, wears a brimmed hat, coat, waistcoat, and breeches.
Whilst these figures seem to pair, the bases are different. If they are a pair, figures must exist with the same bases.
HEIGHT: 6.5 inches
PRICE: Pair: E, Singles: F.

Fig. 1982E
A spill vase and arbour group figure of a boy and girl standing on either side of a goat, he wears a plumed hat, shirt, coat, and trousers and is holding a pipe. She wears a plumed hat, blouse, and long skirt. Below them a sheep and a dog are recumbent.
HEIGHT: 10 inches
PRICE: F.

Fig. 1983A
A spill vase figure of a seated boy and girl, with a
dog above them and two lambs below. The boy,
with his right hand raised to his head and his left
to his side, wears a hat, jacket, and breeches. The
girl, with both arms to her side, wears a hat,
blouse, and skirt.
HEIGHT: 7 inches
PRICE: G.

Figs. 1984E/1984F
A pair of figures of a shepherd and shepherdess seated on rock-
work on rococo style bases. The shepherd, holding a crook in his
right hand and his left resting on the head of his dog, which is
standing on its hind legs with his paws on his knees, wears a hat,
jacket, shirt, and breeches. The shepherdess, holding a lamb under
her right arm with her left resting on rock-work, wears a hat,
bodice, long skirt, and a scarf around her shoulders.
HEIGHT: 8 inches
PRICE: Pair: E, Singles: F.

Figs. 1984M/1984N
A pair of Parr figures of sleeping
shepherds, both rest with one arm
on a tree stump with crooks on the
ground. Each shepherd's dog is
recumbent on the base, a sheep and
a lamb rest on the base of her figure.
He wears a shirt with tie jacket and
knee breeches. She wears a jacket
and skirt with an apron.
HEIGHT: 6.75 inches
PRICE: Pair: E, Singles: F.

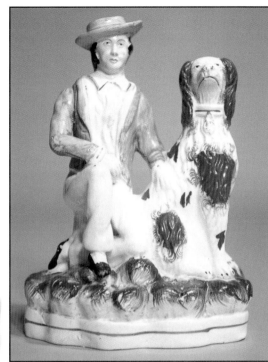

Figs. 1985/1986
A pair of figures of a kneeling woman and man. She is wearing a brimmed hat and a long dress with an underskirt. To her right is seated a large goat. The man is wearing a brimmed hat, jacket, shirt, and trousers. A large dog is seated to his left.
HEIGHT: 8 & 8.5 inches
PRICE: Pair: D, Singles: E.

Figs. 1986A/1986B
A pair of figures of a boy and girl seated on rock-work on rococo style bases with filled baskets at their feet. The girl, with her left arm round a goat and her right feeding it, wears a headscarf, bodice, and skirt. The boy, with his right hand resting on the head of a dog and his left holding a bird, wears a headscarf, ermine edged cloak, shirt, and breeches.
HEIGHT: 6.5 inches
PRICE: Pair: E, Singles: F.

Fig. 1997B
A group figure of a girl seated under an arbour decorated with flowers, wearing a plumed hat, bodice, jacket, and shirt with an apron. Her left arm is around a bird, which sits on her lap, and her left rests on the head of a dog that has its forepaws on her apron. Below there is a small bridge under which a stream flows.
HEIGHT: 10 inches
PRICE: G.

Figures were also made of dogs accompanying their master or mistress in the farmyard or even on their fishing boats.

Fig. 2015J
A standing figure of a girl wearing a brimmed hat, blouse, open sleeved jacket, and skirt holds a bag of fruit in her right hand and a large sheaf of corn in her left. A dog sits at her feet.
HEIGHT: 9 inches
PRICE: F.

Fig. 2009C
A spill vase figure of a girl leaning against a tree trunk wearing a hat, blouse, jacket, and a skirt with an apron. She is holding a basket of fruit in both hands. A dog sits at her feet. **The strange hat the girl is wearing appears on a number of figures. The authors have been told that it is of Welsh origin, but know of no evidence to confirm this.**
HEIGHT: 7 inches
PRICE: G.

Fig. 2016B
A spill vase group figure of a boy seated with a girl standing below. She wears a blouse and skirt and has one arm around the boy and the other on his knee. He wears a brimmed hat, open neck shirt, jacket, and trousers, holding a bird in his right hand and his left is around a dog that has its forepaws on his lap.
HEIGHT: 6.5 inches
PRICE: G.

Fig. 2016C
A group figure of a boy standing on rock-work wearing a plumed hat, jacket, and kilt while holding a garland in his right hand. A girl stands below wearing a hat, bodice, and short skirt. Her right hand is on her hip and her left holds a bird aloft. A dog sits by her feet.
HEIGHT: 8 inches
PRICE: H.

Fig. 2016D
A spill vase group of a boy kneeling and a girl standing on a bridge, below which a swan is swimming. The boy wears a plumed hat, cloak, blouse, and kilt. At his feet a dog is reclining watching the swan. The girl wears a bodice and short skirt and rests her arm on the trunk of a tree.
HEIGHT: 8.5 inches
PRICE: G.

Fig. 2016E
A group figure of a boy and girl seated on rock-work, he looks down on her and wears a tunic and kilt. A bird is perched on his left arm and his right is around her shoulders. She is bareheaded and wears a blouse and skirt. Her right arm is around a dog that sits on her lap.
HEIGHT: 8.5 inches
PRICE: F.

Fig. 2016J
A group figure of a boy seated on another's shoulders, the boy above wears a jacket, shirt, and trousers; the boy below a blouse and skirt with trousers. Both boys are taking fruit from a tree that is to their left. Below a dog plays and on the ground is a hat with fruit in it.
This is another version of children 'scrumping', that is stealing apples from an orchard or elsewhere.
HEIGHT: 9 inches
PRICE: F.

Fig. 2033F
An arbour figure of a girl seated and a boy standing on either side of a gate. Above the gate is a clock face surrounded by a grapevine in which two birds are perched. The girl wears a jacket and skirt with an apron and her hat is over her arm; the boy wears a shirt with collar, tunic, and knee breeches. A small cloak is over his shoulder and he is holding a basket of fruit in his left hand. Beneath the gate a small dog is recumbent.
HEIGHT: 9.5 inches
PRICE: F.

Fig. 2035A
A group figure of a man and woman standing, she wearing a bodice and long skirt, he in highland attire of Tam O Shanter, tunic, kilt with sporran, shoes, and socks. He has his right hand on her shoulder and they hold between them a large scarf. A dog sits to his left.
HEIGHT: 12 inches
PRICE: F.

Figs. 2051G/2051H
A pair of figures of a man and woman standing, he wearing a plumed hat, scarf, long jacket, waistcoat, shirt, and kee breeches. His dog sits between his feet and he has one hand on his hip and the other holds the top of a fruiting grapevien. Below the vine on a stand is a beehive. She wears a hat with feather, bodice, open sleeved jacket, and a skirt with an apron. There are grapes in the apron and her left hand rests on the top of a fruiting grape-vine. Below the vine, on a stand, is a beehive. Her dog sits at her feet.
A very well modelled and rare pair of figures.
HEIGHT: 10.75 inches
PRICE: Pair: D, Singles: E.

Fig. 2057
A figure of a man seated cross-legged with one elbow resting on a tree stump to his left. He fondles his dog with his right hand; the dog is seated on its hind legs with its paws on its owner's leg. There is a sickle between the man's legs, and a large sheaf of corn by his side. This figure is sparsely coloured, yet well modeled; had it been fully coloured the price paid would be higher.
HEIGHT: 12.75 inches
PRICE: F.

Fig. 2078A
A spill vase group figure of a boy and girl standing on rock-work, he wears an open necked shirt, waistcoat, jacket, and trousers. He has one hand raised to his head. She wears a hat, bodice, and long skirt with a scarf over her shoulders. Both children are watching below where a dog is chasing a cat.
HEIGHT: 9 inches
PRICE: F.

Fig. 2080
A spill vase group figure of a boy seated on a fence and leaning against a tree, a girl standing to the left on a titled base with gilt script, a dog at her feet looking up at the boy, a lamb lies on the base. **This figure is interesting as it is titled "Present from the Lowther Arcade", obviously an enterprising retailer must have ordered a number of figures bearing this title to sell at their premises, and other figures have been seen with "A present from The Thames Tunnel".**
HEIGHT: 6.75 inches
PRICE: G.

Fig. 2082A
A spill vase figure of a woman seated to the side of a tree, wearing a turban, ermine edged cloak, bodice, jacket, and long skirt with an apron. Both hands are in her lap and a dead bird hangs head down from one hand. To the other side of the tree, a spaniel sits on its haunches.
HEIGHT: 10 inches
PRICE: E.

Fig. 2086B
A group figure of a man standing wearing a steeple hat with a scarf attached, shirt, three-quarter length jacket, and loose knee breeches. He carries a basket over his right arm and holds a shotgun by its barrel. His left hand is on the head of a woman who sits next to him wearing a headscarf, blouse, and long dress. Her hand rests on a jug, below which a dog is begging.
HEIGHT: 9.5 inches
PRICE: E.

Far left:
Fig. 2098A
A group figure of a girl and boy standing on rock-work. The girl, with her right hand to her side holding a basket, her left across her waist, and a lamb lying below, she wears a plumed bonnet, jacket, and dress. A scarf drapes across both their shoulders. The boy, with his right arm raised holding the scarf, a dog standing on his knee, and his left hand resting on his hip, holds a plumed hat and wears a jacket, shirt, and breeches.
HEIGHT: 9 inches
PRICE: F.

Left:
Fig. 2100C
A standing figure of a boy wearing a long jacket, shirt with tie, waistcoat, knee breeches, and a cloak over his shoulder. To his right, standing on rock-work on its hind legs with its forepaws on the boy, is a spaniel.
HEIGHT: 7 inches
PRICE: F.

Right:
Fig. 2100E
A standing figure of a man wearing a hat, frilled shirt, waistcoat, and knee breeches. One hand is on his hip and the other is around a spaniel that stands on its hind legs on a fence with its forepaws on the man.
HEIGHT: 6.5 inches
PRICE: F.

Far right:
Fig. 2105C
A spill vase figure of a man standing leaning against a tree, wearing a Tam O Shanter hat, ermine edged cloak, jacket, waistcoat, and trousers with knee boots. His right hand is placed inside his coat and his dog lays on rock-work by his feet.
This is a common figure but it is not known whom it portrays. He is very well dressed and he could well be theatrical in inspiration.
HEIGHT: 13.25 inches
PRICE: F.

Fig. 2105F
A group figure of a girl and boy standing on either side of a table, she wears a plumed hat, bodice, jacket, and skirt with an apron in which she holds flowers. She holds a garland of flowers aloft. He wears a plumed hat, tunic, and kilt and holds a spaniel in both hands. The whole arrangement is upon a shaped and waisted base.
HEIGHT: 9 inches
PRICE: F.

Fig. 2107A
A group figure of a boy standing and a girl seated by a gate, with a dog seated below. The boy wears a plumed hat, shirt, jacket, a kilt with sporran, and a scarf over his shoulder. The girl, with a bird on her lap, wears a plumed hat, blouse, and skirt.
HEIGHT: 10.5 inches
PRICE: F.

Fig. 2106
A spill vase figure of a woman standing cross-legged, wearing a plumed hat, blouse, coat, and long skirt, a scarf over her left shoulder and across her body, holding a rabbit in her right hand, her left rests on a tree trunk to her side, a dog stands on its hind legs below the tree with its forepaws on her waist.
HEIGHT: 10.5 inches
PRICE: E.

Fig. 2107B
A standing figure of a woman wearing a plumed hat, blouse, and skirt with an apron. Her left hand rests on rock-work and her right holds a nest of eggs. In her apron there is a quantity of fruit. A dog stands on its hind legs on rock-work to her side with its front paws in her lap.
HEIGHT: 7.5 inches
PRICE: F.

Fig. 2108
A group figure of a
sailor and girl
standing side by
side, she is wearing
a plumed hat,
blouse, coat, and
skirt with apron, to
the sailor's left at
his feet is a hutch
and a rabbit, on top
of the hutch a dog
stands on its hind
legs with its
forepaws on the
sailor.
**This may be a
version of 'The
sailor's return'.**
HEIGHT: 10 inches
PRICE: F.

Fig. 2108C
A group figure of a man standing dressed in theatrical
attire, wearing a hat with ribbon, frilled shirt with tie,
jacket, knee breeches, and boots. His right hand is on the
head of a dog that stands on its hind legs with its forepaws
on his waist. His other arm is around the shoulders of a
woman who stands on a brick arch under which a swan
swims. She wears a plumed hat, bodice, and long dress
with a scarf over her shoulder and across her waist.
HEIGHT: 11 inches
PRICE: E.

Figs. 2108A/2108B
A pair of spill vase figures—the
vases designed as large flowers—of a
boy and girl standing holding
Poodles in their arms, with pails at
their feet. The boy is wearing a
brimmed hat, shirt, skirt, and a sash
around his waist. The girl is wearing
a brimmed hat, blouse, and an
aproned skirt.
HEIGHT: 9 inches
PRICE: Pair: E, Singles: F.

Fig. 2109
A group figure of a man standing cross-legged, wearing highland attire, to his right a woman is seated with her right elbow resting on a stump and holding a bird. A dog is seated on her lap with its paws resting on the man's chest.
HEIGHT: 10.5 inches
PRICE: F.

Figs. 2111E/2111F
A pair of spill vase figures, the spills in the form of tulips, the figures of a girl and boy seated to the side of the tulips. She wears a hat, shawl, and long dress. A cat stands on its hind legs with its forepaws in her lap. He wears a hat, shirt, jacket, and trousers. A spaniel is recumbent at his feet. To the side of each of them on a stool is a beehive.
HEIGHT: 6.5 inches
PRICE: Pair: E, Singles: F.

Fig. 2110B
A spill vase group of a boy and girl seated on a mound before a tree, both wear brimmed hats, she a jacket and skirt, he a jacket, shirt, and kilt. His right leg rests on the top of a kennel and a dog sits outside it.
HEIGHT: 9 inches
PRICE: F.

Figs. 2111G/2111H
A pair of spill vase figures of a boy and girl seated, both wearing similar dress with a brimmed hat, blouse/tunic, and skirt/trousers. They both sit with their hands in their laps and a dog at their feet. In the spill above them is a bird's nest and perched above is a bird.
HEIGHT: 4.5 inches
PRICE: Pair: G, Singles: H.

Fig. 2112
A spill vase group figure of a man and woman standing on either side of a tree, she is to the left holding a bird and wearing a feathered hat, bodice, and long dress, a scarf over her arm; he is to the right, wearing a plumed hat, tunic, knee breeches with boots, and a long cloak. A dog seated at their feet and below there is a bridge under which two swans swim.
HEIGHT: 11.5 inches
PRICE: F.

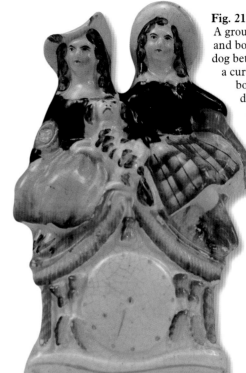

Fig. 2113D
A group figure of a girl and boy seated with a dog between them, above a curtained watch-face, both similarly dressed in plumed hats and blouses, she with a skirt, he with a kilt.
HEIGHT: 6.25 inches
PRICE: G.

Fig. 2113B
A group figure of a boy and girl standing above a clock face, a dog seated to the right of the boy, and the boy has his left arm around the girl's shoulder. He is wearing a hat, neckerchief, shirt, jacket, and breeches. The girl, holding a lamb, wears a hat, blouse, shirt, and bloomers.
HEIGHT: 6 inches
PRICE: G.

Fig. 2113E
A group figure of a boy and girl standing on either side of a clock face, a dog lying on the base between them, both dressed in blouses, sashes across their chests, and a kilt/skirt. This figure can be found both as a clock face and a watch holder.
HEIGHT: 9.5 inches
PRICE: F.

Fig. 2117
A spill vase group figure of two children seated, wearing highland clothes, beside a tree trunk with a dog between them, below a brick wall and train. HEIGHT: 10 inches PRICE: E.

Fig. 2126E
A group figure of a fisherman seated on rock-work with his right hand to his eyes, peering into the distance. He wears a brimmed hat, open neck shirt, jacket, and short trousers, with a net over his shoulder. Below him a woman sits bareheaded with a scarf over her shoulders wearing a bodice, jacket, and long skirt. She holds on her lap a bowl that contains eels, at her feet a dog sits, and all on an arched gilded base. **This figure was made by The Parr factory.** HEIGHT: 11.5 inches PRICE: E.

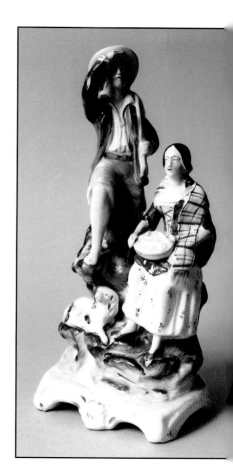

Fig. 2126F
A group figure of a boy and girl on a bridge. He is seated she standing, both similarly dressed in a blouse and kilt/skirt. A dog sits on the boys lap with its forepaws on the girl. Beside both of them is a basket filled with fish. A rod rests on the ground with its end in a stream that runs below. HEIGHT: 8 inches PRICE: G.

Fig. 2120
A group figure of fisherman standing in a boat with a net over his shoulder, in the boat a dog is seated on a barrel. Beside the fisherman is his wife seated on rock-work holding baskets of fish in each hand. HEIGHT: 9.75 inches PRICE: E.

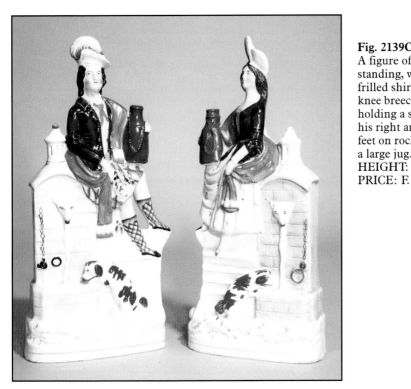

Fig. 2139C
A figure of a boy standing, wearing a hat, frilled shirt, jacket, and knee breeches. He is holding a spaniel under his right arm and at his feet on rock-work stands a large jug.
HEIGHT: 8 inches
PRICE: F.

Figs. 2138/2139
A pair of figures of a man and woman seated above and on fountains, from which water flows through an animal's head, a dog drinks from the water in the trough at the bottom. The man is wearing a plumed hat, short jacket with a scarf over his shoulder, and kilt, she is wearing a plumed hat, bodice, and long dress with a scarf around her. They both hold pitchers, he in his left hand, she in her right.
These figures had as their inspiration the 'Pure water fountains' that were installed by public subscription and charities to wean people away from the ale houses and gin palaces, for at the time it was thought healthier to drink beer and spirits rather than the dubious water obtainable.
HEIGHT: 13.25 inches
PRICE: Pair: D, Singles: F.

Fig. 2139A
A figure of a boy standing, wearing a long jacket, frilled shirt, breeches tied at the waist, and a scarf is over his shoulder and under his arm. He is holding a pitcher on his right shoulder with his left hand. A spaniel sits at his feet. To his other side is a small fence.
HEIGHT: 7 inches
PRICE: F.

Figs. 2145/2146
A pair of standing figures of a man and woman, both holding bottles on their shoulders, he is wearing a short jacket, shirt, and knee length trousers with boots, a scarf tied around his waist, a dog standing on hind legs to his right with its forepaws on his waist, she is wearing a short jacket, blouse, and long skirt with a scarf over her right arm, a sheep standing on its hind legs with its front legs on her waist. By the side of each figure is a brick well from which water flows.
HEIGHT: 9 inches
PRICE: Pair: E, Singles: F.

Fig. 2180
A figure of a man standing, wearing a hat, coat, waistcoat, and knee breeches with leggings, he carries a bundle of faggots on his shoulder and another under his arm. Over his right arm he carries a bag and in his hand a chopper. A dog is seated by his left leg.
This figure is known as 'The faggot gatherer'.
HEIGHT: 14.25 inches
PRICE: E.

Fig. 2181
A figure of a standing woodchopper, one foot raised on rock-work, wearing a hat, long coat, waistcoat, and knee breeches with leggings. Over his left shoulder is a large net bag and suspended from the other a small box and in his left hand is an axe. A dog is seated on a raised rock-work to his left.
This figure has been incorrectly restored, the net should be larger.
HEIGHT: 14 inches
PRICE: E.

Fig. 2181B
A spill vase group figure of a boy chasing a rabbit; he wears a cap, shirt with tie, jacket, and knee breeches. His left hand holds his cap as he leaps over a style. His dog is below, chasing a rabbit that is running into a culvert.
This is a very rare and well modelled group and is from the same factory or modeller who made Figs. 2661/2662. It is possible that there is a pair to this figure, but it is as yet unrecorded.
HEIGHT: 9.75 inches
PRICE: E.

Index

A

Alsatian, 90

B

'Billy the Rat', 124, 129
Bulldogs, 122
Bull Mastiff, 90

C

Campbell, Thomas, 182
Children with dogs, 134-177
Clock face figures, 174, 244, 252

D

Dalmatian, 91-92
'Dog Tray', 182-183
'Don't you wish you may get it', 127

G

Game Dogs, 93-107
'Gerlert', 177

K

'King of Sardinia', 181

M

'Maida', 178
'McGrath', 77
'Mother Hubbard', 183

Q

Queen Victoria, 181

P

Pekinese, 108-109
Poodles, 110-118
Pugs, 119-123
Pipe smoking dogs, 124-125
Pure water fountains, 253
'Pretender', 77
Prince Alfred, 179
Prince of Wales, 134-136, 179-180
Princess of Wales, 134-136
Prince Albert, 179

R

'Royal Stag Hunt', 179

S

Scot, Sir Walter, 178
Spaniels, 19 - 27, 54, 56-73
Spaniel Jugs, 55-56
Spaniels on bases, 40-53
Spaniels with flower baskets, 35-39
Spaniels with pups, 44-49
Spaniels with separate legs, 28-35, 39, 41-46, 49-53, 66-67
Spaniel tobacco jar, 54
Spaniel window jamb, 54
Spaniel Begging, 55
Spill Vase Dogs, 125, 129

Spill Vase Figures, 39-40, 71, 75, 77, 81, 83, 86, 89-90, 94-97, 105, 110, 125, 129, 138, 143, 145, 150, 152, 156, 161, 163-164, 167, 169, 171, 173, 175, 182, 186-187, 190-191, 193, 195-196, 201-207, 209-210, 212, 216, 221-222, 225, 228, 230-231, 234-236, 239-240, 242-243, 246-250, 252, 254

T

'The faggot gatherer', 254
'Toby', 128

U

Unidentified breeds, 124-133

W

Watch holder figures, 76, 177, 185, 204, 218, 235
Whippets, 74-79, 82-87, 89
Whippets with spill vase, 75, 77, 81-82, 85, 89
Whippets with quill holder, 79-81, 87

Victorian Staffordshire Figures 1875-1962. Adrian & Nicholas Harding. Since the 1960s, the best Victorian Staffordshire ceramic figures pieces have achieved values rivaling porcelain figures from Dresden and Meissen. Over 350 beautiful images here display the figures produced from 1875 onward at their best, both original pieces and later reproductions. The Parr-Kent Factory; Sampson Smith; James Sadler & Sons, Ltd.; Lancaster & Sons, Ltd.; Joseph Unwin & Co.; and Arthur J. Wilkinson, Ltd. are shown to have made figures ranging from portraits to a menagerie of animals. Among the famous personages represented are Queen Victoria, Robert Baden-Powell, Winston Churchill, Horatio Nelson, and Woodrow Wilson. The informative text gives tips on determining original figures from reproductions, brief histories of the Staffordshire factories involved, and important information on values, with value codes in the captions. This is a wonderful companion volume to the author's three previous informative texts on this subject, covering the period 1835-1875.

Size: 9" x 12"   326 color & 29 b/w photos 172 pp.
ISBN: 0-7643-1799-7   hard cover $59.95

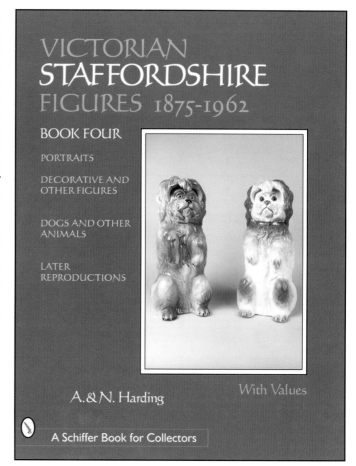

Schiffer books may be ordered from your local bookstore, or they may be ordered directly from the publisher by writing to:
Schiffer Publishing, Ltd.
4880 Lower Valley Rd
Atglen PA 19310
(610) 593-1777; Fax (610) 593-2002
E-mail: Info@schifferbooks.com

Please visit our web site catalog at *www.schifferbooks.com* or write for a free catalog. Please include $3.95 for shipping and handling for the first two books and $1.00 for each additional book. Free shipping for orders $100 or more.

Printed in China